CLAWHAMMER
COOKBOOK

TOOLS, TECHNIQUES & RECIPES FOR PLAYING CLAWHAMMER BANJO

MW00817595

BY MICHAEL BREMER

ISBN 978-1-4803-3832-6

HAL•LEONARD®
CORPORATION

7777 W. BLUEMOUND RD. P.O. BOX 13819 MILWAUKEE, WI 53213

In Australia Contact:
Hal Leonard Australia Pty. Ltd.
4 Lentara Court
Cheltenham, Victoria, 3192 Australia
Email: ausadmin@halleonard.com.au

Visit Hal Leonard Online at
www.halleonard.com

CONTENTS

INTRODUCTION

This is the golden age of learning music. There are hundreds of books and videos that teach basic technique and tunes. The Internet is filled with songs and tunes that you can learn. You can even take private lessons with some of the world's best players through webcams. In fact, there are so many great resources available to the learning musician that an instructional writer like me has to think long and hard to answer these questions:

- With all that music instruction out there—much of it for free—what would make a truly useful book for banjo students with instruction that they can't find elsewhere?

- What could I add to the literature that would really help players learn to play better and enjoy it more?

I didn't see a need for another book filled with dozens or even hundreds of tunes. There are plenty of those books out there already. I didn't see a need for another book that taught how to play a specific style like Round Peak, or how to emulate a particular player like Tommy Jarrell or Wade Ward. There are already enough teachers and materials out there teaching that. What I wanted to do was to help banjo players learn more about their instrument—how to develop their skills, ears, and technique in ways that can be applied to every tune they learn. And rather than teach how to play like someone else, I'd like to give you the tools, techniques, and examples to develop your own personal style.

When the good folks at Hal Leonard Publishing suggested that I write something in their *Cookbook* line, it all gelled. Like cooking, banjo playing is a matter of combining basic ingredients in different ways using various techniques, adding some spice for interest, and experimenting and improvising to take each dish—or tune—to a new level. So, using the metaphor of cooking, I could guide players to explore the kitchen (learn the neck), introduce different flavors (tunings), add spices (licks), and hone "cooking techniques" to experiment with the music, learn how to improvise with different flavors and methods, and develop their own style.

So, after slaving over a hot banjo for a long time, here it is. Yes, there are a number of tunes in this book, but for most of them, we'll dig in and play each of them in two, three, four, or more ways, with the goal of showing you different ways to approach and play any tune you like.

WHAT IS CLAWHAMMER?

Since the title of this book is *Clawhammer Cookbook*, I guess I should give the definitive definition of clawhammer-style playing. Sorry, but I can't. I've taken many workshops where this was discussed, and I got a different answer every time. I've spent far too much time scouring the web for words of wisdom and just ended up where I started. If you're interested, do a search on "clawhammer vs. frailing" or "clawhammer vs. Round Peak" to see hundreds of pages of semantics that make sense from all sides.

For the purposes of this book, we'll define clawhammer very generally as playing banjo with a downstroke technique. This means that (for the most part) you'll be hitting down on the strings with the back of the fingernails as opposed to plucking up on the strings as you would in the classical or Scruggs styles.

So clawhammer is the overall term for this style of playing. Various techniques and patterns within the style include the good ol' bum-ditty, double-thumbing, and drop-thumb, among others, all of which will be defined (to the best of my ability), explained, and used to make music.

TRADITION

Tradition is a wonderful thing. We all owe a great debt of gratitude to people like Alan Lomax, Mike Seeger, Brad Leftwich, and all the other collectors, teachers, and players who preserve, teach, and perform our musical heritage in the way it was played in the past. I have and will continue to learn from the masters—in person when possible, and otherwise through books and recordings.

A lot of traditional music developed in isolated communities where tunes and techniques were handed down through the generations. Many players can tell (and play) the differences in styles between different counties in North Carolina. And that's fascinating, delightful, and worth learning. But music, including folk music, isn't static. It always has and always will evolve and change, incorporating new styles, techniques, influences, and innovations. Today, with radio, cable and satellite television, and the Internet, very few of us live in isolated communities. I don't know anyone who grew up exposed only to one type of music. My home and my friends' homes were filled with folk music, but also rock, jazz, classical, Indian, and other types. These sounds, harmonies, and rhythms are a part of us. And, in the tradition of evolving folk music, it's OK if they start to find their way into our playing—even when we play clawhammer banjo!

The trick is to study and preserve the old ways but allow the music to grow and reflect our lives and the world we live in. And again, because we're in that golden age of learning music, we can hear (and sometimes see) the music being played in the older traditional ways. Because everything is being preserved, we have even more freedom to put our own influences into the music and create new traditions.

In addition to taking liberties with technique, you can also take liberties with repertoire. Our heroes of clawhammer banjo, from places like North Carolina, played the music they grew up listening to. This is the music they loved, and that had meaning for them. Because of that love and the meaning, when they played it, it made us love the music and feel the meaning. As much as I love to hear and play traditional tunes, I, along with most of today's banjo players, grew up listening to other styles of music, which have meaning for us. We should play the music that we feel—i.e., sometimes I just gotta play a Grateful Dead or Beatles song that was important to me in my youth!

I believe that music is an important tool in forming bonds between people. Shared music is as important as shared food and other shared traditions in social situations. I think we should play the music that builds community. I regularly attend old-time jams, but I also like bluegrass jams and blues sessions. And many of my friends like to play swing music—I want to play along.

So this book isn't about preserving or duplicating tradition in any particular style. There are other people and books and videos that teach that. This book is about playing music on the banjo—any music, all music. For legal and monetary reasons, the music presented here is all traditional or written for this book. But the techniques shown here can be applied to many styles of music. You may be surprised—happily, I hope—that clawhammer fits well into a number of musical styles outside of the tradition.

PRESENTATION

Speaking of tradition... traditionally, old-time clawhammer banjo evolved to accompany the fiddle at dances. Banjo was the rhythm section, keeping the beat, hinting at the harmony, and playing a simplified version of the melody. Solo clawhammer banjo is a relatively new twist; but it's a good one. Playing fiddle tunes solo on clawhammer banjo requires a fairly accurate version of the melody. And if you play the tune a few times through, each time should be at least a little different—i.e., different ornaments, different rhythmic accents, and even improvised counter-melodies.

Also, old-time music traditionally has no solos. Everyone plays the melody (or whatever you want to play) together. That's one of the things I love about old-time jams; they're very democratic. You get to play all the time and not just wait in the background until it's your time to step forward and take a solo. Everyone works together to make the music. And that's wonderful... in a jam session.

But today, in a performing string band, solos are part of the music. So are dynamics. Depending on the size, style, and skill of the band, there may be times when you, as the banjo player, have to play simpler music to allow the soloists or vocalists room to improvise. You may need to reduce your volume to allow the singer's voice or a soloist's instrument to be heard without screaming or over-playing. To support singers and soloists, sometimes you may play just the chords or sometimes a counter-melody. You may want to play in different registers (higher up or lower down the neck), depending on the solo instrument, to add contrast and avoid clashing. And there may be times when you will be expected to take a solo, so you'll need to play fancier. If you're playing all-out the whole song, you'll have no way to step it up for your solo!

So, for each song or tune, it's good to know:
- A clean, simple way to play the chords, possibly in more than one register.
- A slightly fancier way to play the chords, with fills and/or bass lines.
- A clean way to play a simple version of the melody.
- A fancier version of the melody (or alternate melody) for a solo.

You may not use all of these ways every time you play the song or tune, but it's nice to have them in your toolbox.

When accompanying yourself or another singer, there are many options. You can play the straight clawhammer simplified melody with hinted chords the whole time. You can play simpler chords during the singing and get fancier during a break or solo. You can play a rhythmic groove the whole time or break out of it for a solo. As we progress through this book and look at different tunes and songs, instead of learning the melody and moving on, we'll dig into the tune and see how it can be played in different ways.

But whatever you play, how you play it, and whether you prefer to play simply or to get fancy, remember to keep a steady, solid rhythm. Remember that the banjo has evolved in modern times, but it's still made from a drum!

TUNING AND TUNERS

It is important to play in tune—yes, even the banjo. And again there are differing schools of thought here. Some say to always tune by ear and never use an electronic tuner. This is the ideal method: have your ear so well developed that you can tune by ear. Some people are born with a great ear. Others need to develop it through practice.

Some say electronic tuners aren't accurate enough. Well, they aren't perfect, but they're good enough for most people in most situations. If you're playing with the philharmonic... insert your own banjo joke here. Many say it works and saves time and lets beginners get in tune sooner so they don't drive everyone else crazy. Plus, in a noisy jam session environment with five, 10, or 20 people tuning, a fiddle in one ear and a bass in the other, it's nearly impossible to hear yourself. At times like this, a clip-on tuner is the only way to go (unless you have a stethoscope). And on stage, an electronic tuner enables you to quickly check or change your tuning, so you don't stop the show and let the guitar player fill the time with banjo jokes.

PREREQUISITES: WHAT YOU NEED TO KNOW TO BE READY FOR THIS BOOK

Yes, this book is meant to be useful for beginners through advanced players. No, it is not a lesson in how to hold a banjo for the first time. To get the most from this book in the shortest amount of time, you should first know:
- How to tune your banjo.
- How to play some basic chords: G, C, D, D7, A, F, Am, Bm.
- How to play a bum-ditty or bumpa-ditty.
- How to play the chords to a song or two.
- How to read tablature (even if it's very slowly).

If you're totally new to any of these things, you can still learn this stuff, but things will take a little more time. Be patient. If you have questions, be willing to stop and look for help from a friend or teacher.

HOW TO USE THIS BOOK

I've organized this book with the idea that the reader could start at the beginning and work through until the end. In other words, first learn the basics and then apply them. But it's your book, your brain, and your life. Start anywhere you want; learn what you want in any order you want. Take what interests you now, or could help you with something you're trying to do now, and leave the rest for later.

One more thing to point out: unless otherwise noted, all examples in this book are in open G tuning.

TUNES AND VERSIONS

Most of the tunes and songs in this book are old-time and/or traditional. Because these melodies have been handed down generation to generation—usually by memory without being written down or recorded—they have changed over the years. Tunes that spread across the country diverged in different ways in different places. If you look, you'll find many different versions of just about every tune that's been around since before audio recording.

The versions of the tunes in this book will most likely vary a bit from the versions with which you may be familiar. This is intentionally done partly to avoid infringing on other people's work, but mostly to show how you can take a familiar tune and add your own touches to make it your own, yet still remain relatively true to the tune.

ABOUT THE ACCOMPANYING CD

Most of the examples are on the accompanying CD to help you better understand them. Because of time and space limitations on the CD, repeats are left off of many of the examples, and just the second endings are played (unless there's something particularly fun or tricky in the first ending).

★ CHAPTER 1 ★
BASIC INGREDIENTS

TYPES OF BANJOS

Banjos come in many shapes, sizes, and styles. Traditionally (way back), old-time banjos were homemade with skin heads and gut strings. Today, most of us have store-bought banjos from either a big manufacturing company or a small shop.

Banjo Heads

Today, we have the option of skin or various formulations of Mylar heads. Skin heads have that really traditional plunky sound but are more expensive, harder to change, and more sensitive to temperature and humidity changes. Mylar is brighter in tone (some think too bright), but they're cheap and nearly indestructible. Mylar heads are available with different coatings as well, each of which has a slightly different sound and feel. Fiberskyn is a Mylar head with fibers molded in to deaden it and give it a plunkier sound. Renaissance and Elite heads have a tone and brightness somewhere between Fiberskyn and plain Mylar.

Open or Closed Back?

Traditionally clawhammer was played on open-back banjos, because that was all that was available, all they could afford, or all they could build. As some of the early greats started earning money from their music, they bought themselves fancy Gibson closed-back banjos.

Today, most of the clawhammerers I'm aware of seem to play open backs. They generally have a mellower, sweeter tone, and they're not as loud, so they blend well in small groups. If you need the volume or want that super bright tone, then you may want a closed-back banjo.

Strings

Most banjos I see around have steel strings—usually medium gauge (as opposed to the light gauge that bluegrass pickers prefer). But nylon, gut, and new formulations somewhere in-between have been gaining in popularity as of late, and I see more and more of them every year at music camps.

To Fret or Not to Fret?

Early banjos, especially home-made ones, were fretless, because it was less expensive to buy and easier to build at home. Fretless banjos have a great sound, and allow for great slides and even quarter-tones. Fretless banjos are best (in my humble opinion) for traditional old-time, with little or no chording and rarely playing above the fifth fret. When playing a fretless instrument, you have to be very precise with your fingering to play in tune.

Fretted instruments aren't much more expensive these days, and are, in many ways, easier to play. As long as you're behind and reasonably close to the fret, you'll play in tune. If you play lots of chords and/or like to play up the neck, then you probably want frets.

Tone Rings

The tone ring is the part of the banjo over which the head is suspended, and it helps to give the banjo more tone and volume. Tone rings can be cast bell bronze, brass rods, wood, or anything in between. There are dozens of options, and they all sound like banjos. So really, they all work, but they each sound a little different. Like most things banjo, tone rings are a personal preference.

Bottom Line

Ultimately, play the banjo that makes you happy. It should feel and sound good enough that you want to play it all the time. If you're looking for a new banjo, play as many different banjos as you can. Note the strings, head, and tone ring of the ones you like the best, and let that narrow down your search.

The only real requirement is that it's a five-string banjo. There's a lot of music for four-string banjos, too—both tenor and plectrum—but for the clawhammer style and sound, you need that fifth string.

LEARNING TUNES

Ideally, we'd be able to hear a tune once and then know it, remember it, and be able to play it. That's a lofty goal to pursue and one that very few of us will accomplish. I know I won't. So, what's the best, fastest, and easiest way to learn new tunes? My glib answer is this: whatever works best, fastest, and easiest for you.

Try different ways and see what works for you. What works best for me is to listen to a tune enough that I have it in my head and I can hum it. Then I find the notes on the banjo and play it over and over and over. Then I'll know it!

Also, use the tools that are available. If you have someone willing to sit with you and show you how to play a tune, use that resource. Of course, that's not always a possibility. If you have a recording, then you can listen to it a line at a time and pick out the notes. There are a number of useful programs and apps that slow music down without changing the pitch to make it easier to figure things out from a recording. If all you have is tab, use that. And if all you have is standard music notation, use that!

In a related issue, there's an ongoing minor controversy: is tab good or evil? There are reasonable arguments for both sides of the issue.

Tab is great in that it's cheap, compact, and easily accessed without other people or electricity. A book or notebook filled with tab gives you nearly instant access to hundreds of tunes.

Tab is bad in that it doesn't give all the small nuances of playing. On the other hand, that can also be a good thing. I sometimes like to learn a tune from tab (or standard notation) without ever hearing it played by someone. The tab gives the outline of the melody, and I can put my own touches on it. And hopefully, I can sound original while still being reasonably true to the tune.

Tab is also bad if you use it exclusively at the expense of developing your ear. Learning by ear helps you develop your ear and your memory—both important parts of being a musician.

Personally, I think the important thing is to learn the tune. How you learn it is up to you. What works best for you? And what is available to you?

TAB VS. STANDARD NOTATION

When you use standard notation for banjo, you first identify the note and then process (in your brain) where on the banjo that note can be played. Most of the time, there's more than one place to play a note. Tab is more direct. It tells you where to put your fingers on which string to play the note. It's clean and clear; there are no sharps or flats to worry about. There's one less mental calculation to make for each note. So, many players who like to learn from written music prefer tab.

That said, it's still useful to be able to read standard music notation. There's a lot of great music in many different styles and genres—and originally written for other instruments—that is available in standard notation and not in tab. If you can read standard notation, a whole world of new music opens up to you.

When I say "read standard notation," I don't mean you have to be able to *sight read* at full speed the first time you see it. Just be able to figure it out one note at a time. You may find it useful to convert it to tab, note by note, until you get comfortable with it.

KEYS

While fiddle tunes are generally played in a particular key because that's what works best on fiddle, songs can (and should) be in any key that works for the singer. And if you're playing solo, you can play tunes in any key you want. So if you have a minstrel-style banjo that's tuned down to open E or even open D, and you want to play a G tune, go ahead and play it in E or D. I promise lightning won't strike!

WARM-UP AND SHAKE OUT

It never hurts to warm up a little before you practice or play. Stretch, flex, and shake your hands; then rub them together to build up a little heat. Move your neck and shoulders to loosen them up. Start practicing or playing slowly and speed up as your hands loosen up.

Monitor your tension. If you build up tension in your hands, jaws, neck, or shoulders when you play, then stop every few minutes and shake your hands, rotate your shoulders forward and backward, and slowly move your head in a circle (both ways) to stretch and loosen your neck.

HOW TO PRACTICE

I've read many opinions on this, and it's all over the map. The only thing I can say for sure is that it's better to practice even 10 or 15 minutes every day than to practice for six or more hours once a week. We learn more that way; it's just the way our brains work.

To this end, I suggest that you create an "official" practice space. It doesn't need to be big and fancy. All you need is:

- A comfortable chair or stool that you can sit on—preferably one where you can put both your feet flat on the floor and that allows (or helps) you to sit up straight.

- A music stand—and it's worth it to invest the $20–$30 for a decent, sturdy stand that can hold books and papers and won't tip over every time you look at it.

- A good light that illuminates your practice space.

- A small table, bookshelf, or even floor space where you can stack the music sheets and books that you're currently working on and keep your tuner, capo, and various picks.

- An instrument stand or wall hanger.

- A metronome (optional but recommended).

If you can, leave the space set up at all times. Have your banjo on the stand or the wall hanger—out of the case—at all times. Make it as easy as possible to sit down and practice when you have five, 10, or 15 minutes to spare. Don't make it a chore to get started. Don't give yourself excuses. Have your space and instrument ready, and when the time's free, sit down and start pickin'.

Better yet, try to establish a time when you'll sit down every day and practice. This is hard for a lot of people, because we all have busy lives. But it's only for a few minutes, so if you really want to learn, try to make it happen. What works for me is to practice every morning with my cup of coffee. I wake up, make a cup of coffee, take it to my practice spot, and start. Sometimes I work on new pieces for upcoming gigs, sometimes I work on learning from different instructional books, sometimes I work on new arrangements of pieces I want to play, and sometimes I just play for the joy of it. But I do it every day. It's a habit. If I'm busy, it might be only five minutes. If I have the time, it may last an hour or more. But I do it every day, with very few exceptions.

If you don't live alone (you're a banjo player… what are the odds of that?), then you may have to negotiate the space with your loved ones. I lucked out and married a woman who must be nearly deaf and blind because she puts up with my looks and my banjo playing on a daily basis.

PRACTICE SPEED

We all want to play fast. But if you can't play something cleanly and musically at a slow speed, it won't sound good fast. Practice exercises and tunes slowly until you can play them smoothly and musically, and then worry about speed.

METRONOMES

As a banjo player, you often fill the role of the drummer in a band. In bluegrass and old-time, there is no drummer, and it's up to you to keep the time and drive the music. So it doesn't hurt to spend some time playing with a metronome.

RECORD YOURSELF

For one of the greatest learning—and humbling—experiences in music, record yourself playing solo. What sounds fine in a band or group setting is one thing, but when you play solo, the microphone picks up every click, squeak, grunt, timing delay, missed note, wrong note, and even correct notes that don't ring clearly enough. You'll hear how you really sound and how much you still need to practice a tune before you perform it.

★ CHAPTER 2 ★
PREP WORK

HOLDING THE BANJO

In spite of the famous song, holding the banjo on your knee isn't practical. To play sitting down, set the round pot of the banjo so it's between your two upper thighs. That'll hold it steady. Tilt the neck up until it's comfortable for your fretting hand (your left hand if you're right-handed, and right hand if you're left-handed).

I find that wearing a strap, even while sitting, helps to keep the banjo steady, so I don't have to worry about holding the neck still while I play. One more thing: you may want to angle the banjo away from your body in such a way as to leave some open space behind it. Those of us with convex guts have a tendency to close off the back of the banjo, deadening and quieting the sound if we hold the banjo too close to ourselves.

Then again, there may be times when you want to cut your volume a little: if the singer has a soft voice, or if you want to play a duet with a quiet instrument like a ukulele. Then jam your belly into the pot and hold it close!

HAND POSITION

If you want to take a lesson from classical players (banjo and guitar), who are the end-product of hundreds of years of technical study, you'll keep your thumb centered on the back of the neck with your wrist as straight as possible. This position allows the most freedom for your fingers to move on the fretboard, and is the best way to avoid injury.

However, very few old-time players have anything to do with rigid classical technique. I find that, for comfort and relaxation, I move my hand in many positions: thumb on back, thumb sticking up, or in between.

However you position your hand, the most important thing to do is to keep as little bend in the wrist as you can. The more you bend your wrist, the more strain there is on your tendons. This makes it harder to move your fingers and causes health problems in the long run. You can get carpal tunnel syndrome from playing banjo with bad hand position.

Whether sitting or standing, try to keep that wrist straight. It may involve angling the neck up. No, it doesn't look like a rock star with his guitar (or banjo) down at his knees, but you won't look cool with your arm in a sling, either.

SITTING, STANDING, AND COMFORT

I do most of my practicing sitting down and most of my performing standing up. Sitting is comfortable and lets you angle the banjo so you can clearly see your fingers on the fingerboard. Standing looks and feels more dynamic and energetic and is generally more entertaining for the audience. But if you only practice while sitting, when you go on stage and stand, you'll find that your hand positions are different and you can't see the fingerboard as well. If you're a performing musician who stands on stage, then consider putting in some practice time while standing.

Some banjos weigh a lot, and when they're suspended on one shoulder, they put a lot of sideways pressure on your spine. That can lead to back problems over the years. If you have a heavy banjo, practice mostly sitting down, but practice standing up enough to be comfortable when you perform. You may also consider trying different straps. I like the springy neoprene kind. Some friends prefer the kind that distributes the weight on both your shoulders. You can also look for a lighter banjo if it's still a problem.

FINGERS

In clawhammer style, the striking hand (the right hand if you're right-handed) strikes the strings downward with the back of the fingernail, using either the index or middle finger, while the thumb plucks up on the fifth and other strings. Which finger should you use? If you're starting out with this style, go for comfort. Put your thumb on the fifth string and the nail of your index finger on the first string. If this feels comfortable, start playing with your index finger. If it feels like a stretch, then replace your index finger with your middle finger. If you have small hands, the middle finger may be your best place to start. After a while, switch fingers and see how that feels.

At least one well-known clawhammer teacher has been quoted as saying, "Pick a finger and stick with it!" If your teacher wants you to do that, then do it. I tell my students to learn to use both fingers. That way, if a nail breaks on your favorite finger, you can still play with the other one.

NAILS AND PICKS

If you don't have thick fingernails and play for hours at a time, you can wear a deep groove in your fingernail, which can split. Ouch! Some players like to use a plastic fingerpick, turned around. There are also metal picks made for clawhammer. Some people apply an acrylic nail, and some people coat their nails with brush-on nail hardeners.

My advice is to start with "nothin' but nail" and see how that works. It's just simpler. No extra parts to buy and carry around. But keep an eye on your nail; if it develops a deep groove, change fingers or use a pick to keep it from splitting.

WHERE TO STRIKE THE STRINGS

Unlike bluegrass players who pluck the strings close to the bridge to get a sharp, biting tone, old-time players play farther from the bridge to get a mellower tone. Many strike the strings over the neck between the 17th and 20th frets. Some banjos have this part of the neck scooped out to give you more finger and thumb room when you play there. Try playing in different places to hear the different tones you can get out of your banjo.

INDICATING FINGERS

There will be times in the various exercises and tunes when I'll indicate which finger to use. But only if there might be some confusion or if a particular fingering is easier or demonstrates a useful technique. Here's how I'll indicate which finger to use:

- **Striking hand** (right hand if you're right-handed): t = thumb, f = index or middle finger.
- **Fretting hand** (left hand if you're right-handed): 1 = index finger, 2 = middle finger, 3 = ring finger, and 4 = little finger (pinky).

CAPOS

Open strings are an integral part of the old-time banjo sound. In standard open G tuning, all the open strings are part of a G chord. To have lots of useful open strings to use for other keys—for example, A—you have to either tune all the strings up a step or use a capo. Yes, there are ways to play in any key without a capo, but you lose the open strings and therefore don't have that old-time sound.

Some players prefer not to use capos at all. I like 'em. They save time, and save wear and tear on the strings. In a performance situation, when you need to change keys in a hurry, a good capo is a lifesaver. Also, they give more flexibility in key choice. If you have to play in B♭ or B, and tune up all the strings three or four half steps, you're asking for a broken string.

Something to remember about capos: when you capo up your strings, you have to raise *all* of them, including the fifth string. If you don't have spikes or another fifth string capoing system, have them installed by a banjo luthier. If you don't want to do that, be prepared to tune your fifth string up and down as needed.

★ C H A P T E R 3 ★

COOKING TECHNIQUES

Now let's look at different techniques commonly used in clawhammer banjo. It all begins with the bum-ditty.

THE BASIC BUM-DITTY

The bum-ditty, along with its many variations, is the foundation of clawhammer playing. Here it is in its simplest form.

TRACK 1

0:00

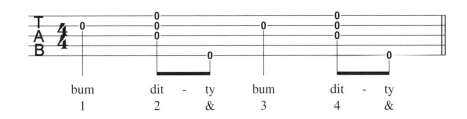

Notice the count: the "bum" starts on beat 1 and lasts a whole beat. The "dit" is on the second beat and lasts half a beat. The "ty" comes in between beats 2 and 3 and lasts half a beat. We often count this as an "and"—i.e., count, "1 and 2 and 3 and 4 and," etc. Then the pattern repeats starting on beat 3. If you're already familiar with this technique, feel free to skip ahead to the next section. If this is new to you, then spend some time just playing the bum-ditty for a while. It wouldn't hurt to count along with it out loud.

Here's how to do it:
1. Hold your striking hand slightly above the strings—no fingers touching the banjo.
2. The "bum": Bring your whole hand down and strike the second string with the back of your fingernail (use your index or middle finger, whichever you prefer), then raise your hand again.
3. The "dit": Again, bring your hand down and brush your finger down and across strings 1, 2, and 3, catching your thumb firmly on the fifth string.
4. The "ty": Bring your thumb up and lightly pluck the fifth string.

Helpful Hints

- Don't rest any fingers on the banjo head; your hand must be free to bounce up and down.

- Don't raise your hand high off the strings—just high enough to clear them.

- When you strike the "bum" and "dit" parts with your finger, don't flick the finger; keep your finger curved and almost stationary. Move your whole hand and forearm up and down as you strike the strings.

- Be as precise as you can with the "bum." Hit just the second string.

- You don't have to pluck the fifth string hard with your thumb. If your thumb is caught firmly on the string, you can just lift it up, and it will make enough sound.

- If this is difficult, and it is for many people at first, then spend a little time practicing just the "dit." Brush your finger across the top three strings and catch you thumb on the fifth string. Do this over and over. Then do it some more.

All you need to play some music is this basic bum-ditty and a few chords. Here's a very basic bum-ditty for "Boil Them Cabbage Down."

TRACK 1

0:09

Boil Them Cabbage Down

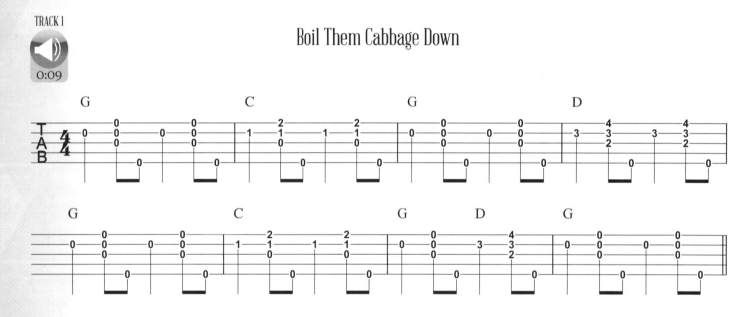

BUM-DITTY VARIATIONS

You can play a lot of music with just the basic bum-ditty, but with a little bit of variation, you can play a whole lot more. The first thing to do is to move your "bum" (no pun intended). To play melodies and get the most out of chords, you have to play the "bum"—the first note of the pattern—on any of the strings. The "ditty" remains the same.

Here, we move the "bum" from the second to the third string.

TRACK 1

0:36

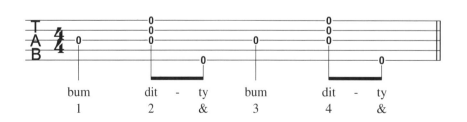

And now, we'll boil them cabbage again, with just this one slight change:

TRACK 1

Boil Them Cabbage Down

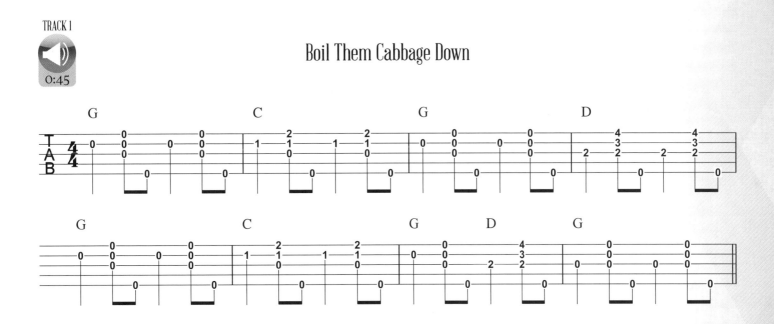

Just moving the "bum" from the second to the third string in a few places really helps to bring out the chords and to hint at the melody. And this is only the beginning. Here are a couple of exercises to help you. Hit each "bum" cleanly and keep a steady rhythm.

TRACK 1

TRACK 1

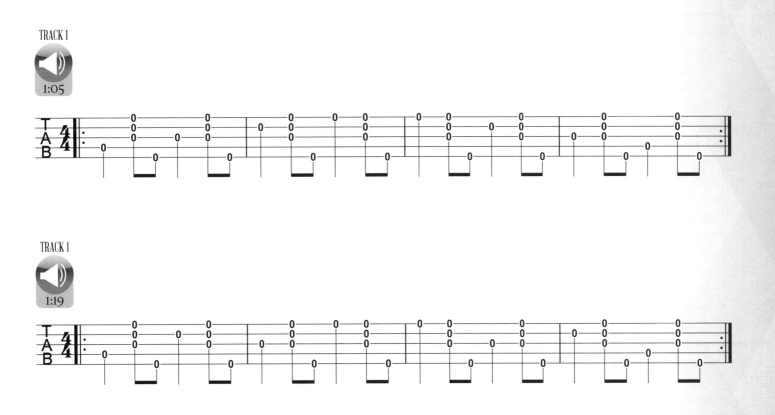

PUTTING YOUR BUM (-DITTY) TO WORK

Now that you can do a bum-ditty with the "bum" on any string, let's play the traditional fiddle tune "Old Joe Clark." It's generally played in AABB form. In other words, play the first half (the A part) twice, then the second half (the B part) twice, then do it again and again (and again). Notice that you play the chords and the melody without ever stopping the steady bum-ditty pattern.

This tune is usually played in the key of A, so if you play with a fiddler, capo or tune all your strings up a whole step. If you're playing solo or just practicing, you can play it in G.

TRACK 1

1:34

Old Joe Clark 1
(bum-ditty)

BRUSHLESS BUM-DITTY

The brush on the "dit" really brings out the chord, but sometimes you don't want or need it. If you're focusing on the melody, for example, you may not want the extra chord notes. And some playing styles, including Round Peak, hardly ever use brushes. Here are some exercises to help you get the hang of it. Slow, steady, and clean is more important than fast.

TRACK 1

2:10

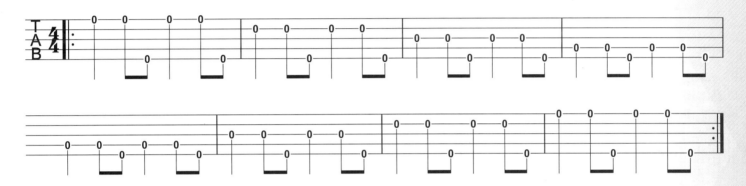

TRACK 1

2:31

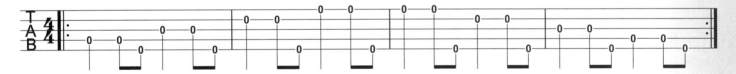

TRACK 1

2:44

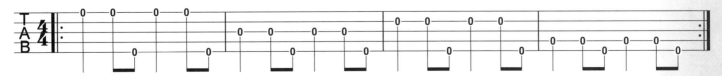

Now let's try "Old Joe Clark" again with brushless bum-ditties.

Old Joe Clark 2
(brushless bum-ditty)

If you're not a purist in any particular style, then you might want to mix brushed and brushless, as in this (yet another) version of "Old Joe Clark."

Old Joe Clark 3
(mixed brush and brushless)

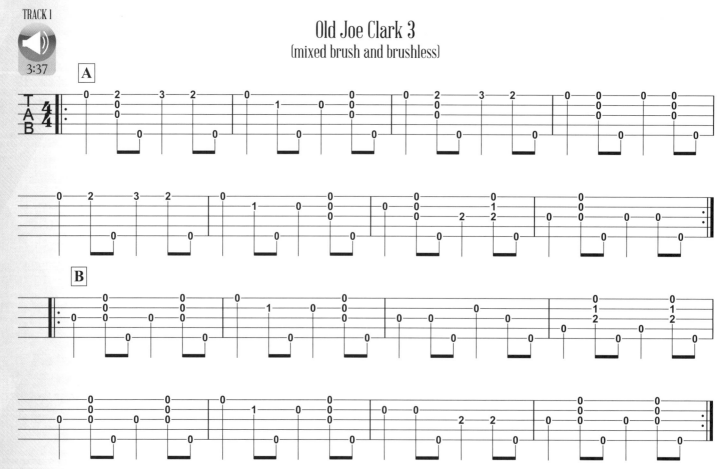

ROUND PEAK BUMPA-DITTY

Because clawhammer is technically a two-finger playing style, we sometimes resort to actually plucking a string with our fretting hand to get an extra note—thereby not disturbing the steady bum-ditty pattern in the striking hand. One way to do this is common in Round Peak playing and is sometimes called the alternate string pull-off.

TRACK 2

0:00

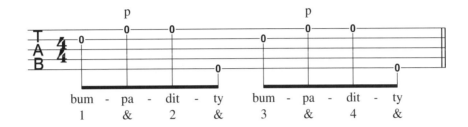

The note ("pa") between the "bum" and "ditty" isn't struck at all with the striking hand; it's plucked or pulled-off by the fretting hand, as indicated by the little "p" above it. Here's the step-by-step:

1. Simultaneously strike down on the second string with the nail of your striking finger AND place your fretting hand middle finger down on the first string, second fret. That's all—strike the second string and put your finger on the first string.
2. NOW pull your middle finger off the first string to make it ring. If you pull it sharply, it'll almost sound as though it was struck.
3. Simultaneously strike down on the first string with your striking finger and rest your thumb on the fifth string.
4. Raise your thumb to sound the fifth string.

This technique provides a steady stream of eighth notes and is a good way to add a little extra "fill" and drive—especially in a part of a song where there's no melody.

DOUBLE-THUMBING

Another way to accomplish the bumpa-ditty is by adding another thumb stroke for the "pa," again providing a steady stream of eighth notes. These exercises will help you get a feel for it.

TRACK 2

0:08

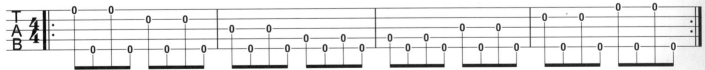

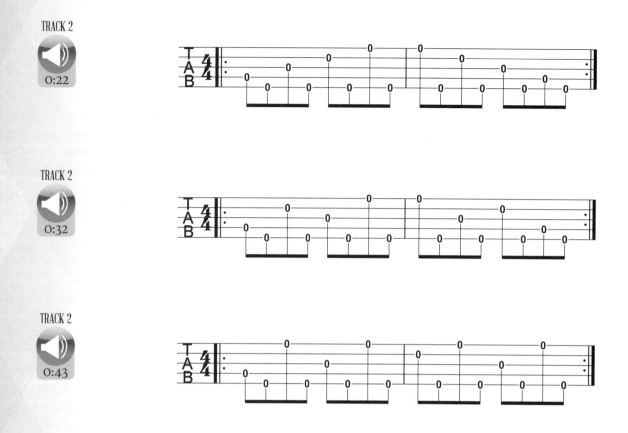

Now let's add some double-thumbing to "Old Joe Clark." Note that it's not used constantly throughout the whole song.

Old Joe Clark 4
(double-thumbing)

DROP-THUMB

The drop-thumb technique opens up clawhammer style to more melodic playing and helps add more interest and variation when playing chords. In drop-thumb, your thumb is freed up to play strings other than the fifth string. It "drops" down from the fifth to the second, third, or fourth string.

Let's start with the double-thumbing bumpa ditty and make one change to turn it into a drop-thumb bumpa ditty.

TRACK 2

1:33

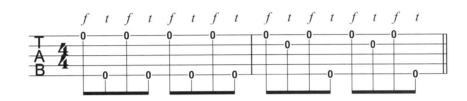

Notice the striking hand fingering: *f* is for finger (whichever finger you decide to use as your "hammer"), and *t* is the thumb. The pattern stays the same in both measures—finger, thumb, finger, thumb, etc.—but in the second measure, the thumb changes between the second and fifth strings.

If this is a new movement for your thumb, take your time and play this two-measure exercise until it feels natural. Then move on to the next set of exercises.

MORE DROP-THUMB

Here are some more exercises to help you get the feel of drop-thumb playing. The first one is a common way to play chords combined with a bum-ditty.

TRACK 2

1:44

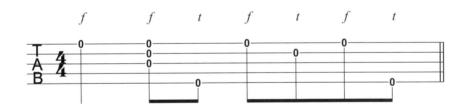

Once you get the feel of this one, try the next one, which moves the "bum" and thumb to other strings.

TRACK 2

1:53

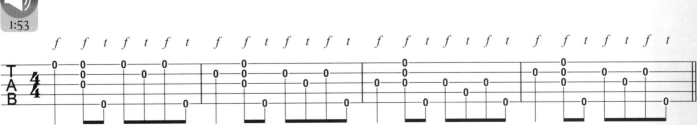

Here's another drop-thumb movement that's useful in playing chords and melodies and helps get more variation in your sound.

TRACK 2

2:08

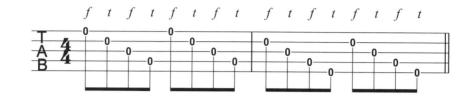

OLD JOE—ONE MORE TIME WITH DROP-THUMB

TRACK 2

2:18

Old Joe Clark 5
(drop-thumb)

HAMMER-ONS AND PULL-OFFS

Hammer-ons and pull-offs are a big part of playing banjo. They let us play notes without having to strike them, and they sound good.

To hammer-on: strike a string (open or fretted) and then "hammer" down a fretting finger on the same string at a higher pitch than the first note. If you hammer sharply, it almost sounds as loud as a plucked note. The first measure below shows hammering-on from the open fourth string to the second fret (on the same string). Notice the curved line (it's called a *slur* in musical terms) connecting the notes and the "h" above it. This tells you that this is a hammer-on. This measure is a bumpa-ditty pattern, with the hammered note on the "pa."

The second measure shows a hammer-on from the second to the third fret of the second string. Again, the hammered note is on the "pa" of a bumpa-ditty.

TRACK 2

2:57

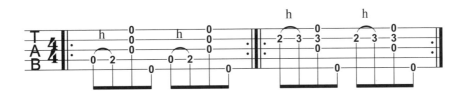

To pull-off: fret a note, strike it, and then pull the fretting finger off the string with enough sideways motion to make the string ring. The first measure below shows a pull-off from the second fret to an open string. Again, notice the curved line and the "p" for pull-off. The second measure shows pulling off from the fourth fret to the second. The pulled notes in both of these examples are on the "pa."

TRACK 2

3:12

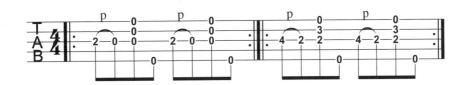

In this next example, there are hammered and pulled notes on both the "pa" and the "ty."

TRACK 2

3:28

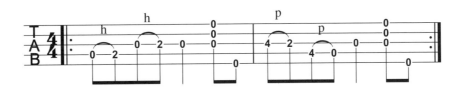

Usually—but not always—hammered and pulled notes occur on the "pa" or "ty" parts of the bumpa-ditty. If you prefer counting, then most of the hammered and pulled notes are on the "ands" in between the beats.

Here's an exercise that uses all the notes that are likely to be in a song or tune in G (i.e., the G major scale) with hammer-ons on the way up and pull-offs on the way down.

TRACK 2

3:39

Here's another little hammer-on exercise that makes use of *unisons*—the same note on two different strings. Using unisons is a very common technique, and we'll come back to them when we hit slides.

TRACK 2

4:05

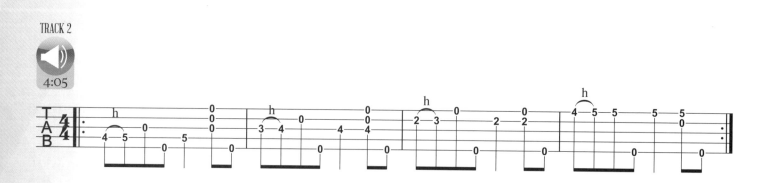

Hammer-ons and pull-offs are so useful and sound so good that you can stick a bunch of them together and make a tune. Here's one I wrote to give you a real hammer and pull workout.

TRACK 2

4:19

Hammered

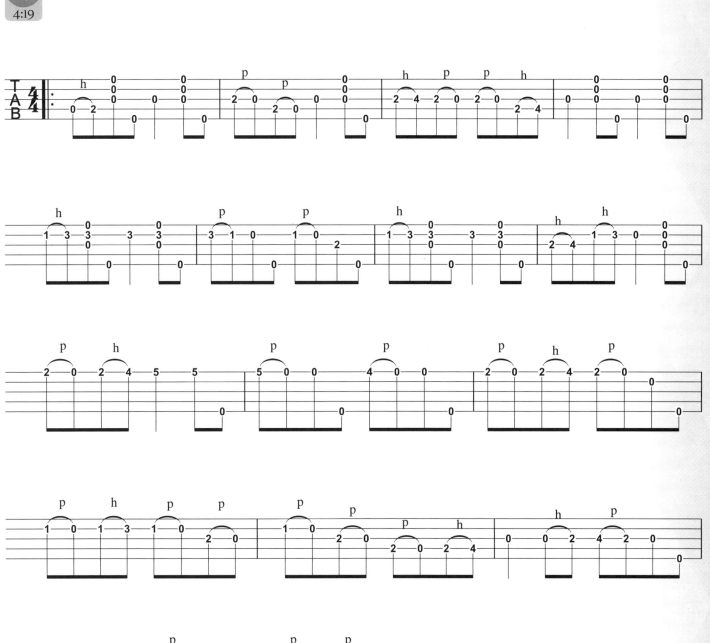

Here's another good tune for working on hammer-ons and pull-offs. "Off to California" is a hornpipe, which has a rhythmic "lilt," so for each two-note pair, play the first note a little longer. You may sometimes see hornpipes written like this, with dotted eighth notes and sixteenth notes:

But often the tab will be all eighth notes, and you'll have to know that a hornpipe is played with a "lilt." You may want to listen to this one on the CD to get a feel for the timing. Note that in the first full measure, you pluck the open third string and then hammer on the fourth fret of the fourth string (without plucking it). Also note that there are a few places, like the very beginning, where you strike once and hammer twice.

TRACK 2

5:07

Off to California

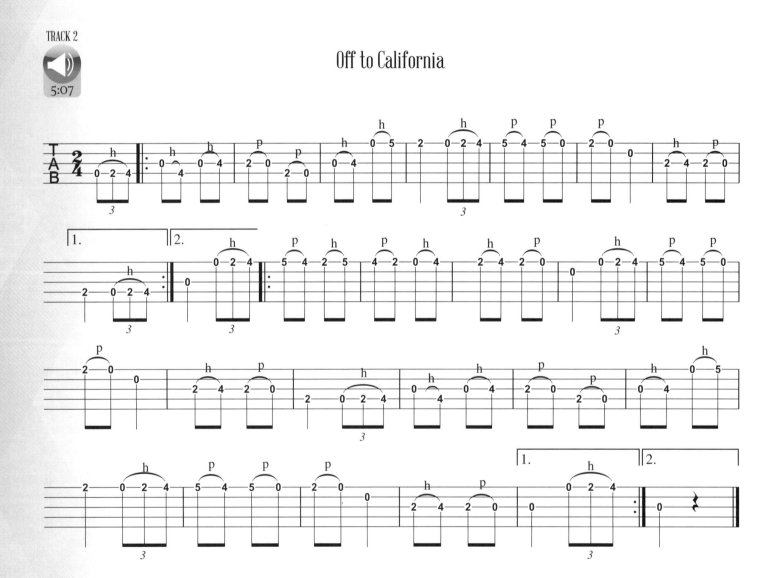

SLIDES

Slides are another way to play more notes and give those notes a different sound. To slide, fret a note, strike it, and then slide the fretting finger up or down to another fret while maintaining pressure against the fretboard.

There's a lot of variation in slides, including how many frets you slide and how fast you do it. Here's an example that shows sliding up to the fifth fret of the fourth string from two places: the fourth fret and the second fret. The "s" and the diagonal line indicate that this is a slide and not a hammer or pull. When you slide, you can either slide fast or slow. I'll play it both ways on the CD.

TRACK 3

0:00

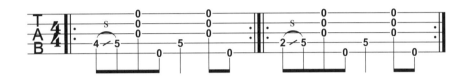

Slides are often slid into unisons, as in this example:

TRACK 3

0:14

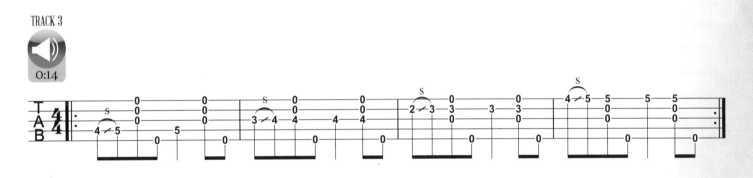

A nice old-time sounding variation of the slide into unison is to slide to the fret just below the unison note and then hit the note on the next string up. Here's an example:

TRACK 3

0:28

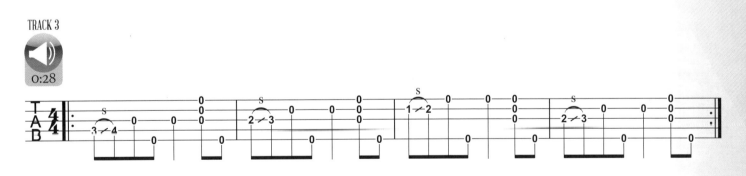

If you have a fretless banjo, then you have even more options for slides—including notes *between* the frets. When you do play those notes between the frets, you have to be careful. There's a very thin line between playing something that sounds great and sounds worse than horrible. If you want to play fretless, it'll help to listen to experienced fretless players to see how they do it.

Here's a version of "Cripple Creek" that uses lots of slides. I wrote out the A and B parts twice each because they're a little different each time. Watch for the drop-thumb in the last measure of the A part, and have fun with the two slides in a row in the fourth measure of B.

TRACK 3

0:42

Sliding into Cripple Creek

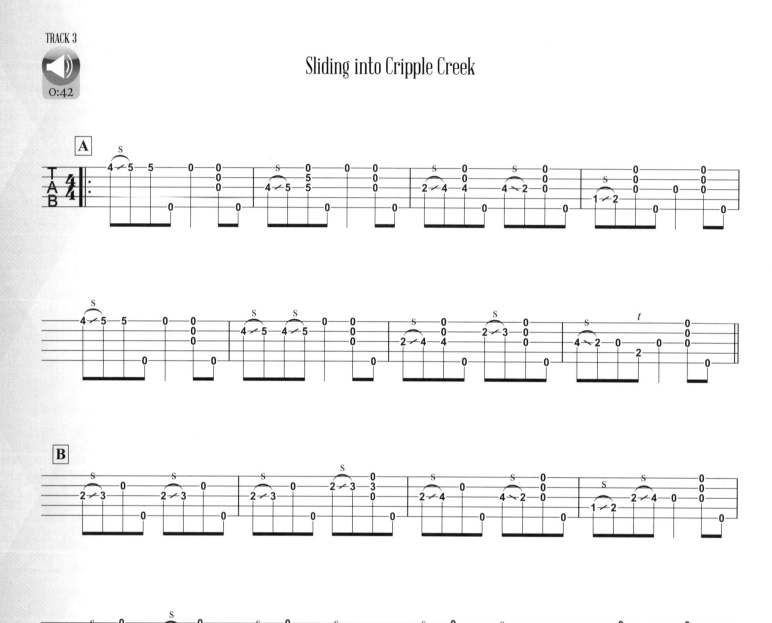

A final word about slides: where you slide from, where you slide to, and how fast you slide are all matters of taste and what sounds best to you in the tune you're playing. Listen carefully to your favorite players and analyze how they like to slide.

SKIP-NOTES

If you skip the "bum," the "dit," or the "ty," you open yourself up to interesting rhythms, longer melody notes, syncopation, and even new styles of music. In this first example, we'll skip a number of "dits." For demonstration's sake, I put in a lot of skips. (This is a technique that can be overused.) Notice how it makes the song sound more delicate. It has less drive, so, for a hard-driving song, don't skip a lot of "dits." But for a softer, wistful song like "Will the Circle Be Unbroken," it seems appropriate. Also notice how the skipped "dits" often happen in places where there's a long melody note, letting you play that full note without obscuring it with a ditty.

TRACK 3

1:23

Will the Circle Be Unbroken
(skipped dits)

Skipping just the "ty" turns a bum-ditty into a swing rhythm. Try playing this typical swing progression found in many songs using a bum-dit. To really get the swing sound, cut the "dit" short.

TRACK 3

2:07

Swing Your Bum
(dits)

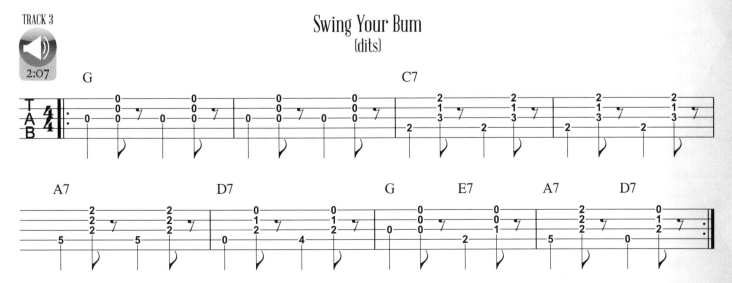

You can throw in a "ty" here and there for fun, but don't hit that open fifth string during the E7 chord (we'll talk more about this later).

You can also get a swingy sound by skipping some "bums" and throwing in a "ty" here and there:

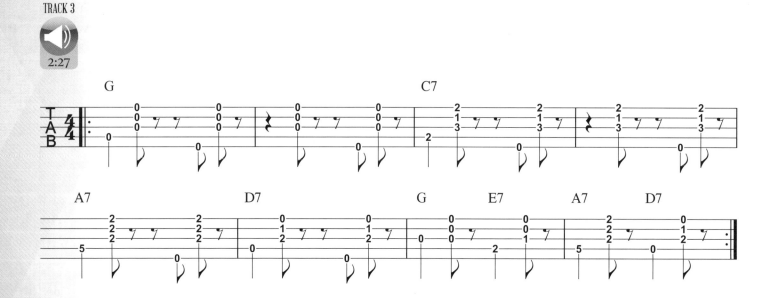

Skipping "bums" can also give you a reggae rhythm. Again, keep that "dit" short.

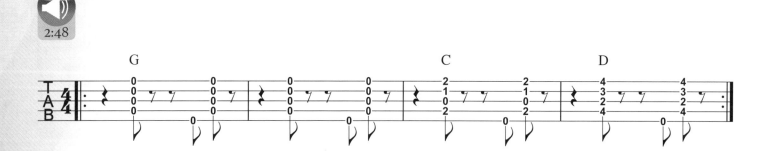

Other Skips

There may be times when you may want to skip a "bum" or two in old-time and folk music as well, especially if you're playing chords. It'll help to break things up. And if you skip both the "bum" and the "ty," then you've got a mandolin-like bluegrass chop.

Some music needs a solid bum-ditty or bumpa-ditty to drive the music, but there are times when skipping a note here and there will add interest, bring out the melody, and give it a different, more delicate feel. Then again, I have a number of "friends" who regularly suggest that I skip the "bum," the "dit," and the "ty" for the whole song!

WALTZING AND GETTING JIGGY

Each bum-ditty or bumpa-ditty takes up two beats. Two of them in a row make four beats, which is great, since most songs and tunes we listen to and play in the Western world have four beats to a measure. So what about waltzes, which have three beats to the measure, or Irish jigs, which have six?

For waltzes, you can usually modify the bum-ditty to bum-ditty-ditty or bumpa-ditty-ditty either for chords or melody playing. You can also skip some "dits."

TRACK 3

3:07

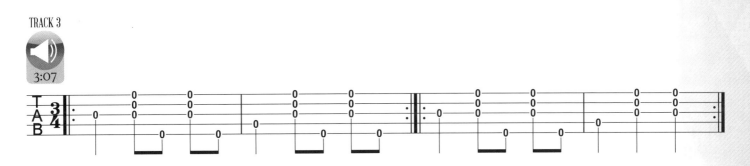

Here's the progression to the traditional waltz, "In the Pines."

TRACK 3

3:25

In the Pines

31

Jigs are in 6/8 time, which means there are six beats to the measure and the eighth note is counted as a beat. Here are a couple of 6/8 patterns. To get the right feel, accent the 1 and the 4.

TRACK 3

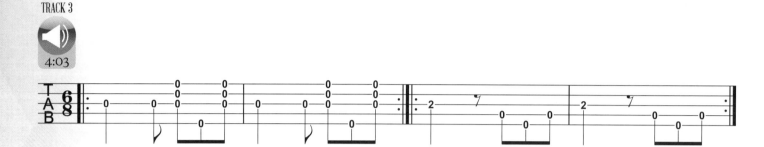

PERCUSSION: THUMPING THE BANJO HEAD

In pursuit of clean playing, many people train themselves to avoid hitting the head while playing. Those who claw up over the neck can't (without some serious contortions), but if you play over the head, you can add a little percussion to your playing.

A good percussionist can bang all sorts of sounds and rhythms out of a banjo head. That's a little beyond the scope of this book, but if you're a drummer or percussionist when not playing a banjo, see what you can come up with. What we will deal with here are ways to incorporate percussive sounds into your playing. Like other techniques, this one is easy to overuse, so pick and choose carefully where, when, and how often you do it.

Of course, an occasional random thump while playing can add some energy or excitement to a tune, but too many random thumps will sound like mistakes instead of effects. There's a thin line between music and noise. To sound musical, the thumping must be rhythmic and fairly regular. Thumps sound different on different banjos, depending on the type and tightness of the head. If you want the thump to stand out more, it might help to deaden the head; try putting a sock in it.

Let's start by using our thumb to add a thump to each "dit" of a bum-ditty. This gives us a drum beat on beats 2 and 4, which are the accented beats in many styles of music (including old-time and bluegrass). This thump should sync well with the strums of a guitar or the chops of a mandolin.

If you're doing your bum-ditty right, then you're bringing your thumb to rest on the fifth string as you brush (or strike) each "dit." You still want to do that, but let your thumb hit and rest on the head as well as the fifth string on each "dit." The "X" below the tab staff lets you know when to thump your thumb.

TRACK 3

Cabbage
(with a dit-thump)

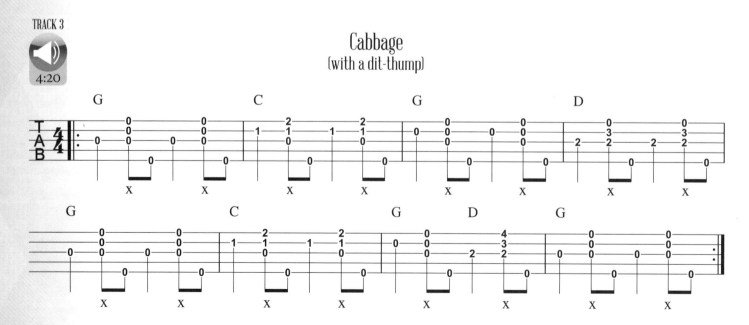

Once you're comfortable with that, you might want to try some double-thumping: thump on the "bum" and the "dit," both with your thumb. As the saying goes, "X" marks the spots.

TRACK 3

4:38

Cabbage
(with bum- and dit-thumps)

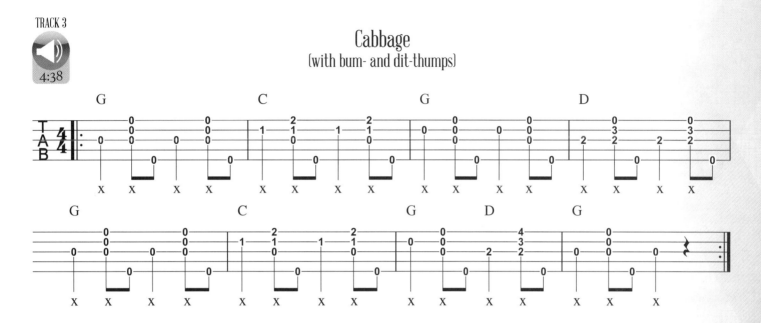

A steady drum beat is good, but sometimes you can't hit all the beats. When you drop your thumb to a string other than the fifth, you can't thump on the "dit." That's OK. Skipping some beats isn't a problem.

TRACK 3
4:58

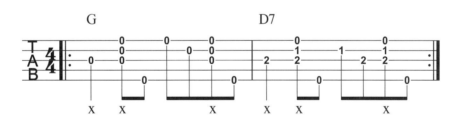

You can also thump with your striking finger. When you hit a "dit," especially on the first string, but also with two- and three-string brushes, you can continue the motion until your finger hits the banjo head. If it's a quick, smooth motion, it'll sound as though it's on the "dit." The "X" above the tab staff lets you know when to thump your finger.

TRACK 3

5:08

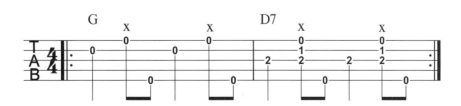

If you combine a double-thump on the thumb (on the "bum" and "dit") and a finger thump on the "dit," you get something reminiscent of a steady kick drum playing four beats to the measure and the snare coming in to accent the 2 and 4.

TRACK 3

5:18

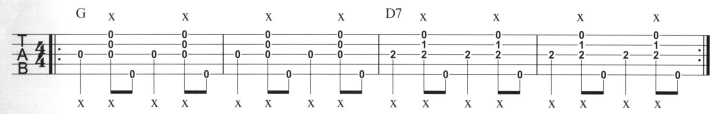

Sometimes you can't play through the strings to hit the head on a "dit" with your finger, especially if it's a single note on the third or fourth string. Then you can thump with other fingers on your striking hand (middle, ring, and/or pinky). Hold them so they strike the head whenever your striking finger hits a string. You may have to play with this for a while to get the feel; try different fingers and combinations of fingers. If you keep your fingers in position, you can thump on the "bum" as well. When you have a feel for it, you can come up with all sorts of variations.

FOURTH STRING "TY"

If you like to play music that has a lot of chords, there will be times when the fifth string drone clashes with the chord. Sometimes that clash is a good thing, adding tension and setting up for resolution. For instance, in the key of G, when you play a D7 chord, the drone G note isn't part of that chord. It doesn't sound "bad," just a little… unsettling. Then, when you follow it with (resolve to) a G major chord, all is right in the musical world.

On the other hand, there are songs (not in old-time, but in pop and swing) where you play the following chord pattern: G–E7–Am–D7. (To really bring out the clash, be sure to hit the fifth string well.)

TRACK 3

5:32

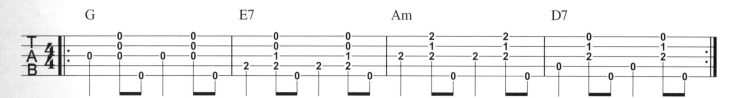

When you play the E7, the drone string sounds bad—not interesting, unsettling bad—just plain bad. So, to keep the bum-ditty or bumpa-ditty (or other pattern) going, when you play the E7 chord, substitute the fourth string for the fifth on the "ty."

TRACK 3

5:46

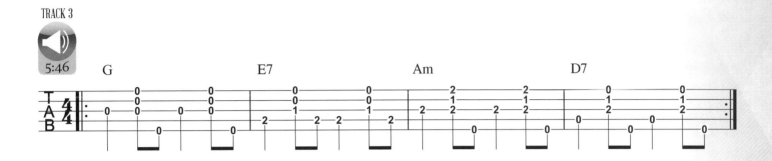

For effect, you can also use a fourth-string "ty" for all four chords:

TRACK 3

6:00

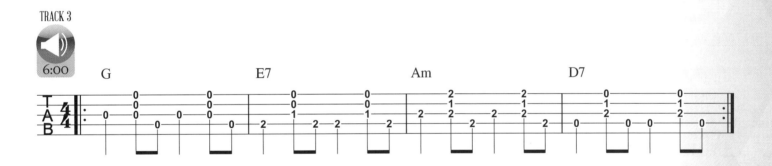

If you really want to keep the fifth string going, then you can play the E7 chord (or any other chord that clashes with the fifth string) up the neck in a way that lets you fret the fifth string to be less offending. Here's one way to do it (there are others). The "1" on the fifth string indicates the first fret above the open fifth string, which is even with the sixth fret of the other strings.

TRACK 3

6:14

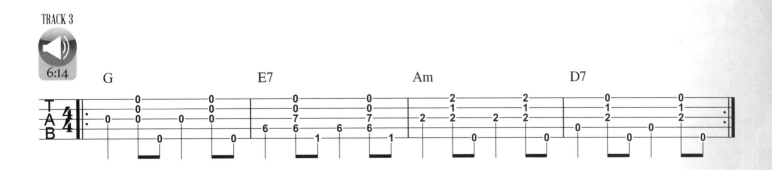

★ CHAPTER 4 ★
LEARNING YOUR WAY AROUND THE KITCHEN

Ever tried to cook in someone else's kitchen? Or have you tried in your own kitchen after your girlfriend or boyfriend rearranged everything while you were out? You waste a lot of time looking for the things you need. It's much easier to cook up some grub when you know where everything is. Likewise, it's easier to learn tunes, especially when trying to learn by ear, when you know where all the commonly used notes and chords are.

This chapter is about getting familiar with the most common notes and chords that you'll need to use when playing clawhammer banjo in open G tuning. We'll look at other common tunings later.

I know this stuff isn't as much fun as playing tunes. And nobody is horribly impressed if you stand up at a jam session and show how you can play a D major scale in G tuning. Furthermore, some old-time players see no need for this stuff; you just play the thing. But knowing your instrument *is* useful. It'll really pay off in time saved down the road. There's no need to get bogged down in this. Explore it a little, move on to different things, and come back every now and then when you feel that it'll help you.

KNOW YOUR STRINGS

Knowing all the notes on your strings can be a great help in playing all kinds of music. It'll help you make chords, find melodies, and change keys. If you love to memorize, then learn all the notes right now. We'll wait for you. Done yet?

For those of us (including me) who aren't enamored with memorization, there are other approaches. At the very least, you need to know the notes of the open strings. They are:

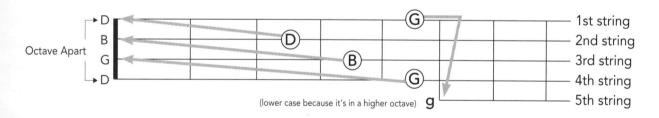

Note that the 1st and 4th strings are the same note, an octave apart, and the 5th and 3rd strings are an octave apart. So there are really only three notes to memorize.

Once you know the open strings, you can figure out any other note on the fretboard when you need it—if you understand the major scale pattern.

THE MAJOR SCALE PATTERN

The major scale—and everyone in the Western world grew up hearing it since before birth, so it's familiar to us all—is a pattern of notes that goes like this:

Whole step - Whole step - Half step - Whole step - Whole step - Whole step - Half step.

The frets on the fretboard are all a half step apart. If you play any note and then play a note on the same string on the next fret up, the new note will be a half step higher. Move to a fret below the original note, and the new note is a half step lower.

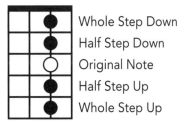

By the way, when we talk about up and down, we mean in pitch. Down is toward the nut and tuners. Up is toward the bridge. So, depending on how you hold your banjo, your finger may be moving downward in the sense that it's getting closer to the ground, but it's moving *up* in terms of the pitch it produces.

It follows that if you go up or down two frets, then you raise or lower the pitch by a whole step. This works on any fret of any string.

One more thing: for some historical reason, the C scale is the starting point for all of this. If you follow this pattern starting from a C, there will be no sharps or flats. Any other starting point (to play in other keys) will have the same pattern, but at least one of the notes will be sharp or flat.

So the notes in a C major scale are:

C D E F G A B C

Then they repeat over and over until only dogs can hear them.

Here's the pattern applied to a C major scale:

What's important to remember is that there is a whole step (two frets) between every two notes, except between E and F and between B and C; those are half steps (one fret).

That's all you have to memorize. So to figure out any note at any fret on any string, you can start at the open string and follow the C major scale up the string until you get to the fret you want.

FIGURING OUT NOTES ON THE FRETBOARD

Let's figure out the note that's on the fifth fret of the third string.

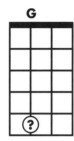

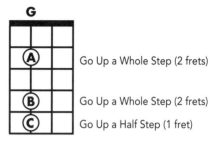

Our starting point is G, because we know that's the note of the open third string. Following the pattern of whole and half steps in the C scale, we start at G, and go up a whole step (two frets) to A; then we go another whole step (two frets) to B. From B to C is a half step, so, we go up one fret, and we're at our destination, which is a C.

That worked out nicely, but what about those frets in between the whole steps? Those notes have two names, either:

1. The sharp of the note below it, or
2. The flat of the note above it.

Let's demonstrate by finding the note on the third fret of the third string.

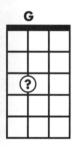

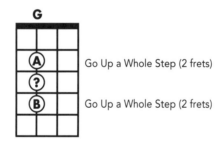

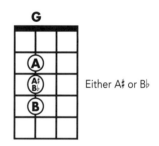

We start as we did before, at G, and go up a whole step to A. Then we go up another whole step to B. But we passed our goal! The note we're looking for is between A and B, so it's either called A♯ (A sharp) or B♭ (B flat). So which one is it? Sonically, these notes are the same on a fretted instrument, so both names work. Practically, use whichever name helps you the most. For instance, if you wanted to make a B♭ chord, calling this note B♭ would be more useful than calling it A♯.

That's really all there is to finding any note on any fret of the fretboard. It'll be a slow process at first, but the more you do it, the faster you'll get, and the easier it'll be.

DO CLAWHAMMER PLAYERS REALLY NEED CHORDS?

Many clawhammer players aren't concerned at all about chords and rarely think about playing them. There's a lot of music to be made by playing a melody offset by the fifth-string drone. And there are some tunes and songs where adding anything else takes away from the mood and the purity of the music.

So, for certain styles of playing and for certain songs and tunes, the answer is no—you don't need to learn chords. But for a lot of music, it's useful to know how to play some chords—both to add some richness to a melody and to play back-up in a band when having the banjo play the melody is too busy.

Even if you don't intentionally play chords, the melodies you play come mostly from chords. So without trying, you're hinting enough chord notes that someone with a good ear can pick them out. Plus, recognizing the chord shapes in the melodies you play can open possibilities and trigger ideas for variations, counter-melodies, and improvisations that will sound good.

So, no, you don't really need chords to play clawhammer banjo—just as you don't really need a knife and fork to eat a meal. It's a matter of choice, preference, and style.

NUMBERING CHORDS

Chords have names like C, D, and E7. But we often give them a number, too. Why? Well, numbering chords does two things:

1. It helps us understand the harmonic function of the chord (OK, this is theory stuff that many banjo players don't care about), and
2. It makes it easier for us to know what chord to play, no matter where the capo is—and this is really useful for banjo players.

Here's how they're numbered for the key of G:

I	ii	iii	IV	V	vi	vii
G	Am	Bm	C	D	Em	F$\sharp$o

Notice that major chords are shown by Roman numerals with capital letters, and minor chords are in lower-case Roman numerals. The diminished chord, indicated with the "o" symbol (which is rarely if ever heard in old-time music), is also in lower case. A couple of common special exceptions are the major II chord (A major in the key of G) and the major ♭VII chord (F major in the key of G), both of which we'll look at soon.

For instance, if you want to play "Boil Them Cabbage Down" in G, you'd play G, C, and D, which are the I, IV, and V chords. No problem. But what if the singer insisted on playing it in the key of B♭? If you think in terms of chord names, you'd have to play B♭, E♭, and F. This isn't impossible, but if you don't regularly play in B♭, it could take a few minutes to figure out the chords.

Now, if you think in terms of I, IV, and V instead of chord names, then all you have to do is slap a capo on the third fret (to bring your I chord, G, up to B♭) and play the I, IV, and V chords exactly as you would in G but with the capo. That's much easier!

Because we banjo players use capos to change keys in many tunings, thinking of chords in terms of numbers can really make our lives easier. If we learn something in one key, like G, we can, with a capo (and some hooks for the fifth string), play that tune or song in 12 keys. Putting a capo on the 11th fret to play in F$\sharp$ may not be the ideal way to play in that key, but it'll work in a pinch.

THE MOST COMMON CHORDS IN THE KEY OF G

The three most common chords in the key of G are G, C, and D (or D7). These three chords are the I, IV, and V chords for the key of G. Here are the most basic ways to play these chords:

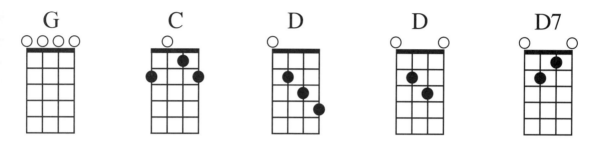

I've shown three options for the D chord, all of which are commonly used and very useful.

Most tunes in G use these three chords. You can play songs for years and never need another chord. But there are many more tunes and songs—and really fun ones to play—that require additional chords.

In the key of G, there are two other relatively common chords: Em (the vi chord) and Bm (the iii chord). A little less common is Am (the ii chord). And just to be thorough, we'll include the F♯° chord, which is rarely used in traditional music but does appear in blues, swing, and jazz.

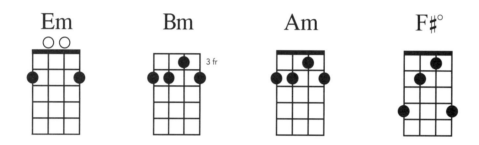

Notice that the Bm chord is the same shape as the Am, just moved up the neck two frets. And notice that the F♯° takes some stretching. If you can't hold it, then just play the notes on strings 1–3 or strings 2–4.

THE II CHORD

We just established that Am is in the key of G, but there are a number of tunes in G that use an A *major* chord. Because it's out of the key, it builds tension (sounds uneasy) but leads nicely to the V chord, which then resolves to the I chord. So when you see an A major in a G tune, it is usually followed by a D or D7, which is then, sooner or later, followed by a G. You'll see this II–V–I chord grouping a lot in swing and jazz as well.

Notice that the A chord is just like a G chord, except two frets (a whole step) up.

Here's the chord progression for the A part of "Redwing" (shown with a simple bum-ditty), which uses the A major chord twice.

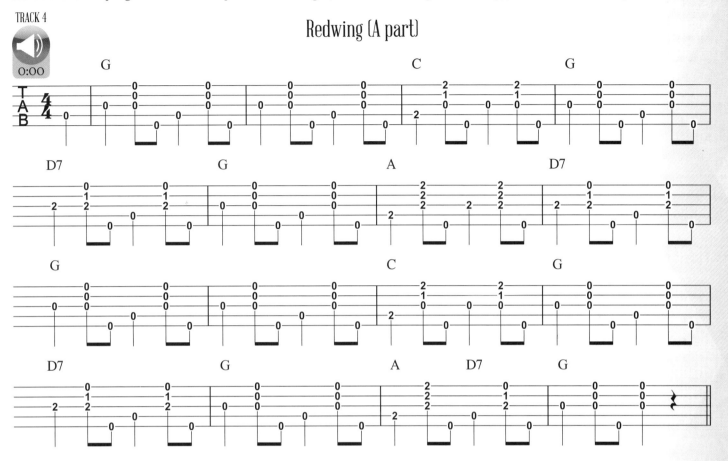

THE ♭VII CHORD

Another chord that shows up a lot is the ♭VII chord. In the key of G, it's an F major, and it's played like this:

F

Many tunes spend a lot of time going back and forth between the I chord and the ♭VII chord—for example, the A section of "June Apple." (This tune is usually played in A; you can capo up and play A and G chords if you want.)

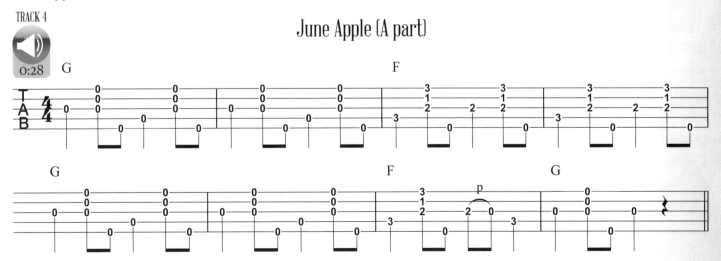

SCALES: USEFUL TOOLS OR TORTURES FROM HELL?

Most of the tunes and songs we play in open G tuning are in the key of G major. The melody notes in that key are all found in the G major scale. If you know the scale—at least which notes are in it and which aren't—then it'll be much easier for you to pick out melodies as you learn new tunes.

Of course, to many players, the thought of playing scales is somewhere between boring and useless and all-out torture. A friend of mine was teaching himself to play guitar and was noodling around, struggling to find the right note. I could tell what he was trying to do and, ever the compulsive teacher, offered to show him a few things that would help him. He emphatically said, "No. I don't want to know about theory or scales or chord construction. I just want to be able to play a note and then play another one that doesn't suck."

After thinking about this for a few seconds, I said, "A scale is a group of notes that, when you play them after each other, usually don't suck." That, it seems, made the concept of a scale acceptable to him. Maybe, it'll work for you, too.

The G Major Scale

Assuming you're still with me, here is the G major scale. There are many ways to play scales. I like to play them like this:

- from G up to the next G
- then back down again to G
- then down as far as we can go with the scale (in this case, to a D)
- and then back up to G

You play all the notes in the scale that you can reach but always start and end with G, which is the root (or tonic) of the G major scale.

TRACK 4

0:45

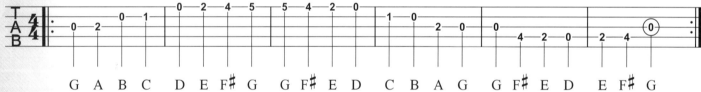

Try to play these notes cleanly and steadily. Start slowly and build up speed over time. If you say the names of the notes out loud as you play them, it'll help you learn them—and the fretboard.

Once you're comfortable with playing the scale, try it in different variations adding a clawhammer touch. For instance, add a "ty" after each note, using this pattern for the whole scale:

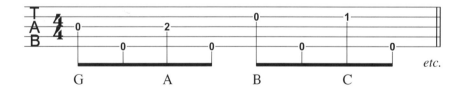

Or use a full bum-ditty pattern for each note of the scale:

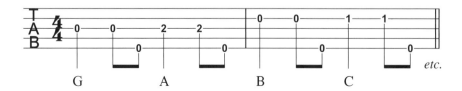

Another way to become familiar with the notes in the G major scale is to harmonize the scale (i.e., add chords). Notice that all the notes in the scale are in at least one of the three basic chords: G (I), C (IV), and D (V).

TRACK 4

1:06

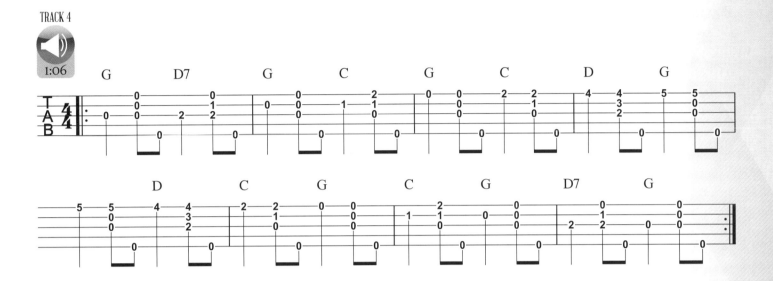

PLAYING IN THE KEY OF A

The easiest way to play in the key of A is to capo all the strings at the second fret and then play as if you were in G. So if you put on your capo and raise the fifth string a whole step to A, then you can play the same chords and scales as you did in G—except it's all up two frets because of the capo, so you'll be playing in A. Try it.

PLAYING THE KEY OF C IN OPEN G TUNING

To play in the key of C, you can capo up at the fifth fret and play as if you were in G or change to a different tuning, like double-C. But you can also play the key of C in open G tuning without even changing the fifth string. The fifth string, being a G, is a drone on the root when you play in G, but it's a drone on the 5th when you play in C. It still sounds good, but it's a little different, and different can be good.

The chords in the key of C are:

I	ii	iii	IV	V	vi	vii		II	bVII
C	Dm	Em	F	G	Am	B°		D	Bb

You already know most of these chords from playing in the key of G. The only new ones are Dm, B°, and Bb.

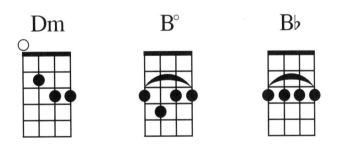

Here's a way to play the C major scale in open G tuning. It goes from the lowest C up to the next C, back down to the lowest C, and then down as far as we can playing the notes in this scale. Because the lowest C on the fretboard (in this tuning) is on the second string, we have to go up the neck to get a full octave. I supplied a possible fretting hand fingering in case it helps.

TRACK 4

1:34

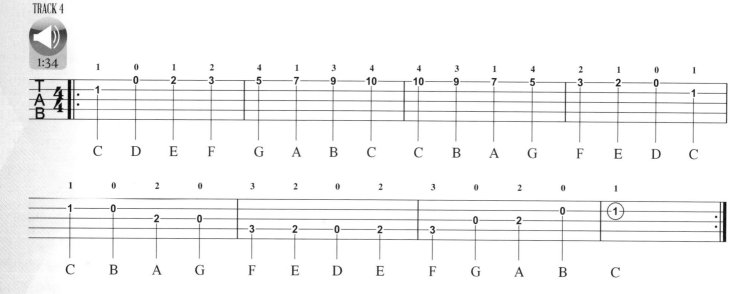

The only note that's different from the G scale is the F—in the key of G, there's an F♯. You can also play this scale with the two additional claw patterns we used on the G scale.

Unless you regularly play in C out of open G tuning, you may not want to spend a lot of time on this. But at least familiarize yourself with the chords and the scale so you'll know that it's here whenever you need it.

PLAYING IN THE KEY OF D IN OPEN G TUNING

Many old-time players only play in the key of D by changing to double-C tuning and capoing up two frets. You can also capo everything up seven frets and play as if you were in G. Or you can just raise the fifth string a whole step to A and play out of (mostly) open G tuning (aDGBD).

Why? Sometimes it's useful. If you're playing at an old-time jam, everyone stays in one key for a long time, and there's plenty of time to change tunings when you do eventually change keys. But in other situations, like a jam in another style of music (bluegrass, blues, and almost anything else), or you're in a band that changes keys every song (or even in the middle of a medley), then it can be very handy to be able to play the key of D in open G tuning. (Yes, you'll need to change the fifth string, but that's a lot quicker than changing three strings and putting on a capo.)

The chords in the key of D are:

I	ii	iii	IV	V	vi	vii		II	♭VII
D	Em	F♯m	G	A	Bm	C♯o		E	C

You already know most of these chords from playing in the key of G. The only new ones are F♯m, C♯o, and E.

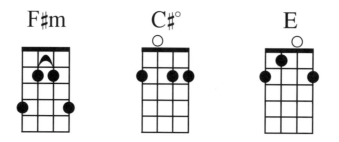

Here's a nice way to play the D major scale in open G tuning (with the fifth string raised to A). It covers two full octaves. I supplied one possible fingering, but feel free to try others. Once you can play this, try it with the two claw patterns we used for G and C.

TRACK 4

2:00

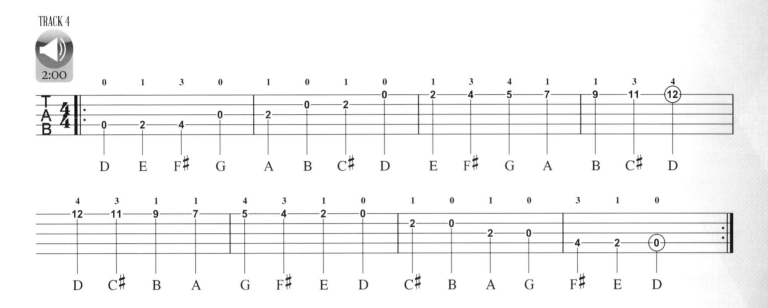

Again, there may be no need to spend a lot of time on this now; just try it a couple of times and know that it's here if and when you need it.

THE STUFF IN THE UPPER CABINET

You can spend your musical life below the fifth fret if you choose, and if that satisfies your musical hunger, then that's great. But if you move up the neck, you open up many new possibilities in your playing. Up the neck, you're in a higher register, so you will blend with or stand out from the rest of the band in different ways. Also, while you may be playing the same chords, up the neck the notes will be in a different order (different chord *inversions*). So while what you play will be "right," it will also be "different." Sometimes different is good. Here are some (but by no means all) additional ways to play the common chords in the key of G up the neck. You don't have to memorize them, but try them out so you can reference them later if you'd like.

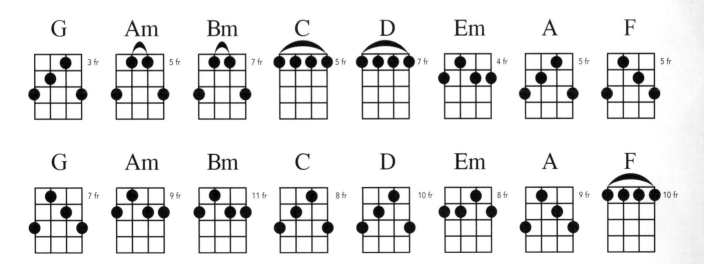

★ CHAPTER 5 ★
MEAT AND POTATOES

Open G tuning, which can be capoed to also be open A tuning (and may other keys as well), is the meat and potatoes of clawhammer music. It's common, but it's tasty and can be used in near-infinite variety.

We'll explore this tuning for playing songs and tunes in the key of G, C, and D. Then we'll capo up two frets to change it to open A tuning and play some music in the keys of A, D, and E. We'll look at a number of ways to play each tune before moving on to the next, trying different techniques that you can apply to any tunes you want to play.

THE KEY OF G IN G TUNING

This is the standard way to play old-time banjo, and many songs are suited perfectly this way. Let's take a look at a few here.

There's No Place Like Home

Be it ever so humble, "Home, Sweet Home" is a great traditional tune that's been around for over 150 years. It was adapted from an opera in the 1820s with lyrics by John Howard Payne and music by Sir Henry Bishop. Let's play this tune in a number of ways. We'll start with a simple arrangement consisting of the melody and a pretty steady bum-ditty with a lot of chord brushes. Note that this tune is played with the "lilting" rhythmic feel discussed earlier (also known as a "shuffle feel" or "swing feel").

TRACK 5

0:00

Home, Sweet Home
(simple melody)

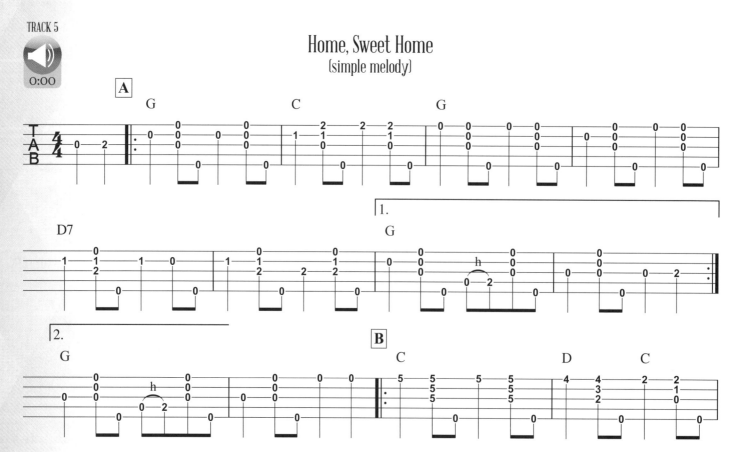

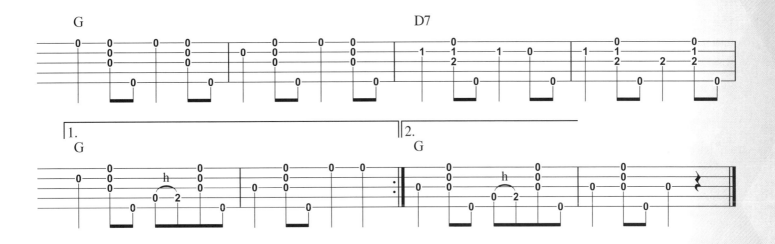

Here's another way to play it. This version uses fewer brushes and some skips to give it a sparser, more delicate sound.

TRACK 5

1:16

Home, Sweet Home
(sparse melody)

There may be times when you back up a singer or instrumental soloist whose improvisation strays far from the melody. At times like that, playing a simple version of the melody may help everyone, including the audience, keep their place in the song. But it may also clash with the improvisation or stifle the solo. So it's useful to be able to play an interesting chord back-up. Here are three ways to play these chords: one very simple, the next a little fancier, and a third up the neck.

TRACK 5

2:34

Home, Sweet Home
(chord back-up 1)

Home, Sweet Home
(chord back-up 2)

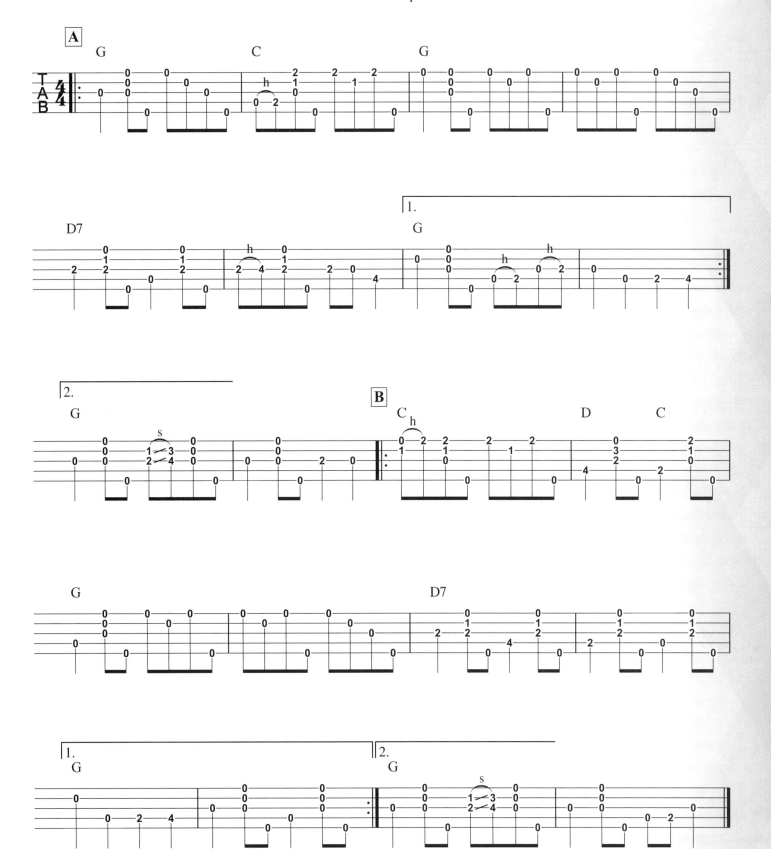

TRACK 5

3:15

Home, Sweet Home
(chord back-up 3)

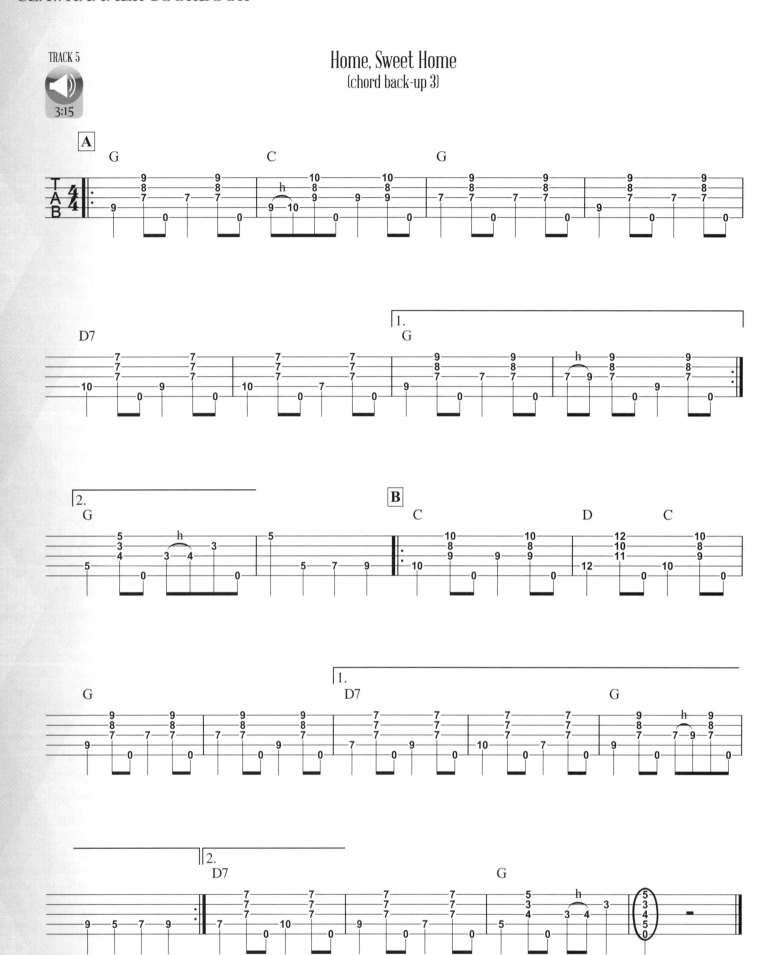

Before we move on, let's try one more thing with this tune: waltz it. Why? Because we can! Sometimes it's a fun challenge to take a tune and change the time signature. I think it makes a pretty nice waltz.

TRACK 5
4:23

Home, Sweet Home
(waltz)

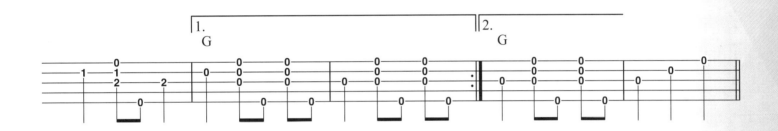

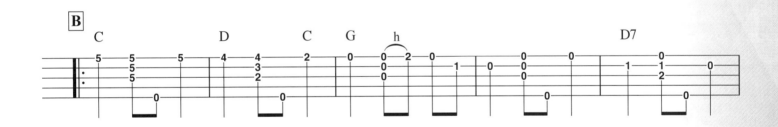

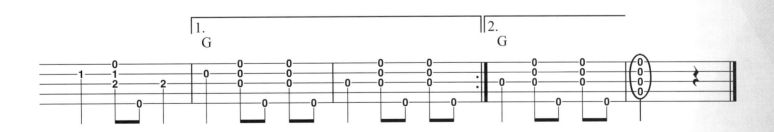

Redwing

"Redwing" is a great crossover song played by old-time, bluegrass, and swing players. Woody Guthrie used the music from "Redwing" for his song "Union Maid." Heck, John Wayne sang "Redwing" in two movies!

While many old-time players don't play many chords—at least not intentionally—most melody notes are in the chords, and sometimes it's easier to play a tune if you hold the chord shapes with your fretting hand. "Redwing" has a melody that plays well from holding the chord shapes. And there's the added advantage of having the other chord notes fingered and ready to go whenever you want to brush a chord. Not to mention that, if you overshoot the string you want and hit an extra string, then any extra notes won't sound too bad if you're holding the chord.

So we'll start "Redwing" by playing the chords first. Watch for the major II chord (in the key of G, that's an A major).

TRACK 5

4:53

Redwing
(chords)

Now let's play a simple version of the melody. At least think about the chord shapes (better yet, actually hold them when possible) and see how so many of the melody notes are in those shapes. Here, watch for the times when you'll use the fifth string as a melody note that's not on a "ty." Also note how skips are used to bring out the longer melody notes.

TRACK 5

5:43

Redwing
(melody)

This version has the melody and some chord brushes. The C chord at the beginning of the B section is played up at the fifth fret.

TRACK 5

🔊

6:31

Redwing
(melody with chord brushes)

Let's try one more version; this time we'll throw in more variations—even a little bit of strumming in a spot or two for emphasis and energy. This one has no repeats (both the A and B sections are written out both times) because each part is different. The "Harm." on the last chord stands for "harmonic." This is a special technique in which you lay your finger directly over the fret wire (fret 12 in this case)—not behind it as in normal fretting, but directly over it—without pressing the strings down to the fretboard. While touching the strings over the 12th fret, pluck them and then quickly lift your fretting fingers off the strings.

TRACK 5

7:33

Redwing
(variations)

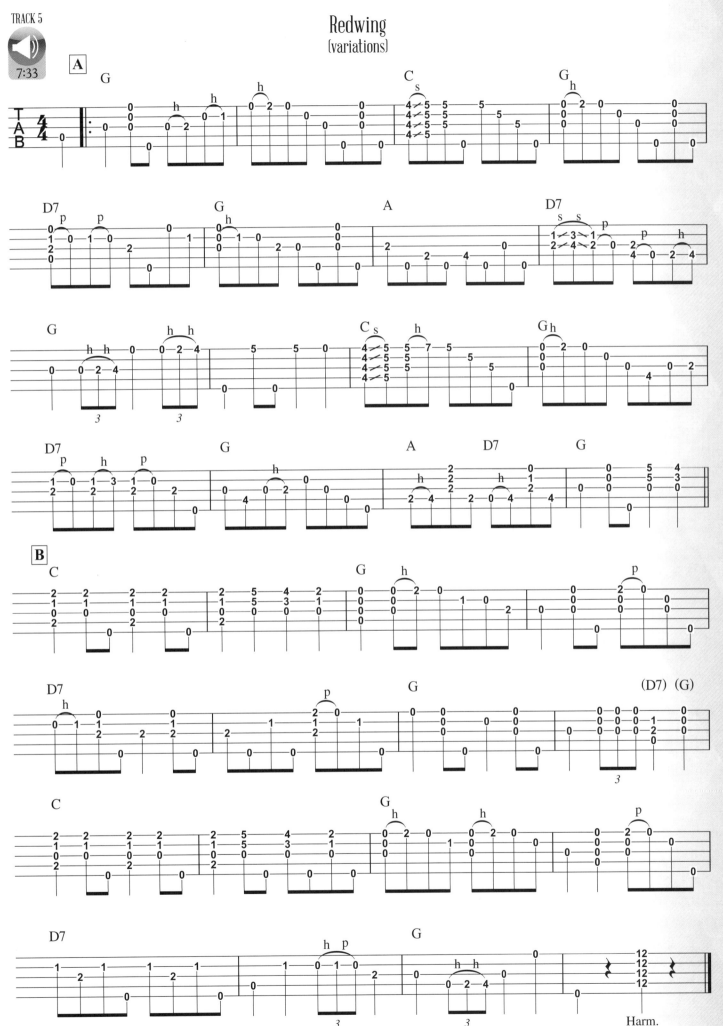

Been All Around This World

Here's an old-time traditional song that's been recorded by many people, including the Grateful Dead. The song has verses and choruses, but the verse and chorus have the same melody and chords. This version has an "extra" measure at the end for a melodic hook; you may prefer to play it without the last measure. Play this one with a shuffle feel.

Let's start with a basic melody and enough chord brushes to bring out the harmony.

TRACK 6

0:00

Been All Around This World
(simple melody)

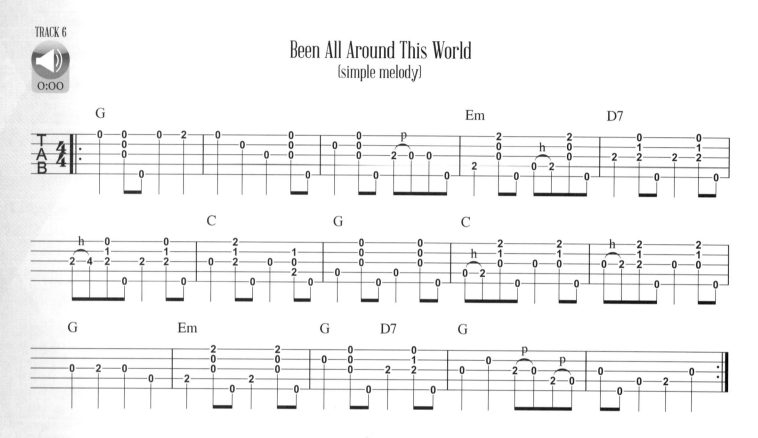

Now let's try a chord accompaniment.

TRACK 6

0:37

Been All Around This World
(chord accompaniment)

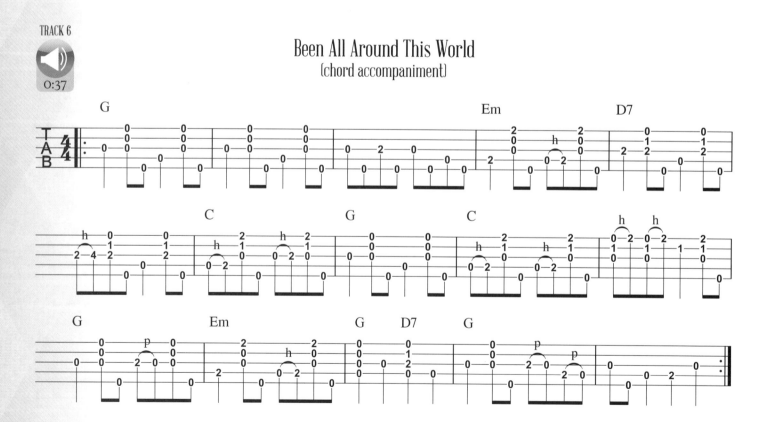

Here's another accompaniment version with chords up the neck.

TRACK 6

1:14

Been All Around This World
(chords up the neck)

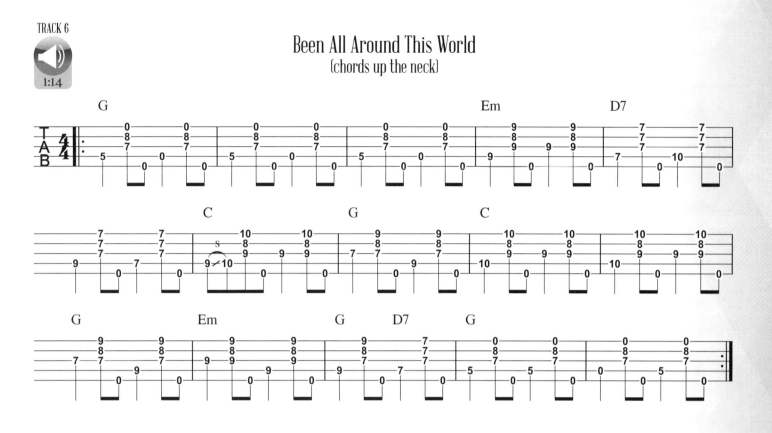

And finally, try playing a full melody up the neck.

Been All Around This World
(melody up the neck)

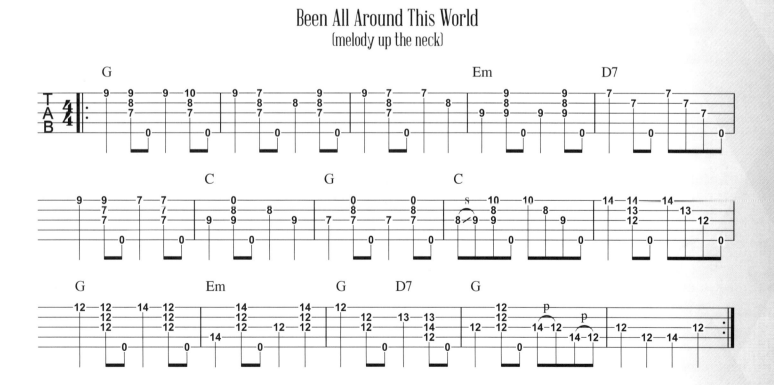

THE KEY OF C IN G TUNING

Open G is a very flexible tuning that works well for pretty much any key. The only limitations are that you may have to retune the fifth string, and you may not have many open strings to play with. Open strings are a big part of the traditional banjo sound (and make playing some things much easier), so many old-time players change tunings for every key. That's great if you have the time between songs to retune, or if you're at a jam where everyone stays in one key for a while. But if you're in a string band that likes to change keys a lot, it's useful to be able to play multiple keys in any tuning.

Dark Hollow

Here's another traditional song that's been played by old-time, bluegrass, and other musicians for a long time. We'll play it in open G tuning in the key of C. Of course, to play this song in C, we could retune to double-C or open C tuning. Or we could stay in open G tuning and capo up at the fifth fret and finger it as we would to play it in G. But for this learning experience, we'll stay in open G tuning and play without a capo. Play this one with a shuffle feel as well.

TRACK 6

1:53

In the second-to-last measure, the melody actually goes down to the C below the low D string. Since we can't hit that note without retuning the string, we'll just jump up an octave to hit that note. In open G tuning, the banjo doesn't have a very wide range. Guitar, fiddle, and mandolin all have more than two octaves easily reachable from open position without moving your hand up the fingerboard. We have barely over one octave reachable from open position. To play two octaves on a banjo, you have to go from the lowest note up to the 12th fret. So we have to jump around the neck to play some melodies that have a wide range.

Also, we tend to run out of low notes, as we did in "Dark Hollow" above. One option is to change the key to one that fits better on the banjo. Another is to play the note(s) an octave up. It won't always sound optimal, but it usually works.

Now here's a mostly chord version of "Dark Hollow" hovering around the fifth fret.

TRACK 6

2:35

Dark Hollow
(chords up the neck)

If you're up for a challenge, try it again playing farther up the neck with more of the melody thrown in.

Dark Hollow
(melody up the neck)

Will the Circle Be Unbroken

Here's a song that almost always works at a jam because a lot of people know it. Bluegrass players often play it in G, but there are times when that key isn't best for the singers, so we'll play it in C. Again, this tune is played with a shuffle feel. Here's a version with a simple melody and enough chord brushes to bring out the harmony, followed by a chord accompaniment.

TRACK 6

3:17

Will the Circle Be Unbroken
(melody)

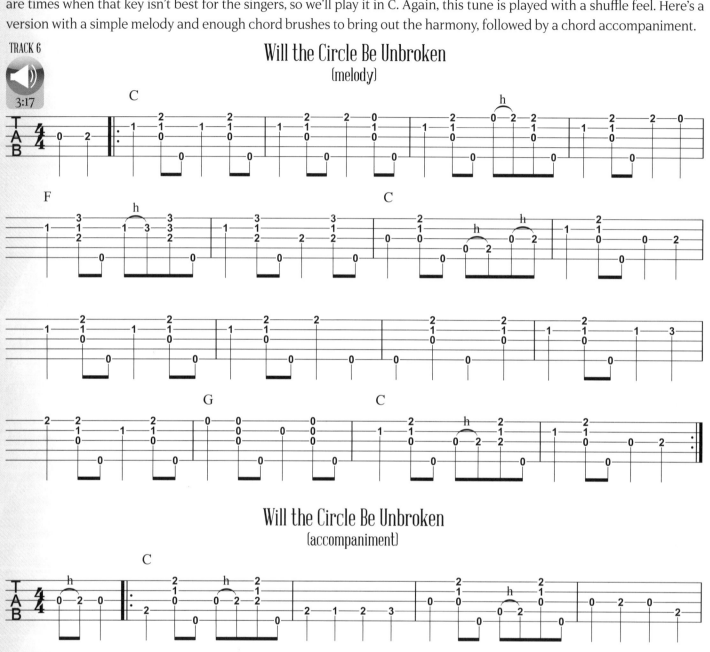

Will the Circle Be Unbroken
(accompaniment)

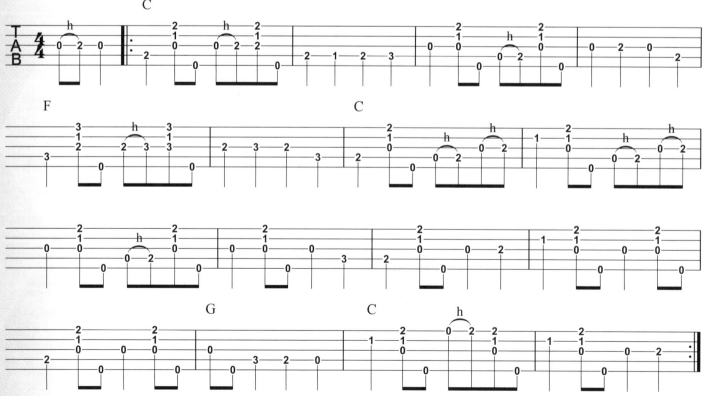

One way to play in C is to put a capo on the fifth fret and play as if you were in G. Another way is to barre that C chord at the fifth fret instead of capoing. There's a little more finger work involved, but it frees you from the capo (if time is a factor) and it lets you use those frets below the fifth. Here's a stab at a melody up the neck that barres at the fifth and moves down the neck for a lick or two. This might make a nice little solo.

TRACK 6

3:57

Will the Circle Be Unbroken
(solo)

THE KEY OF D IN G TUNING

You can also play in the key of D in open G tuning. You do want to tune or hook the fifth string up to be an A. So the drone is the 5th of the key, as opposed to being the root, as it is in open G, which adds a slightly different flavor.

Wreck of the Old 97

"Wreck of the Old 97" is usually considered a country song, but is sometimes played bluegrass style. Let's give it the clawhammer treatment, starting with a basic melody and enough chord brushes to bring out the harmony. This is followed by two more variations.

TRACK 6

4:36

Wreck of the Old 97
(simple melody)

Tuning: aDGBD

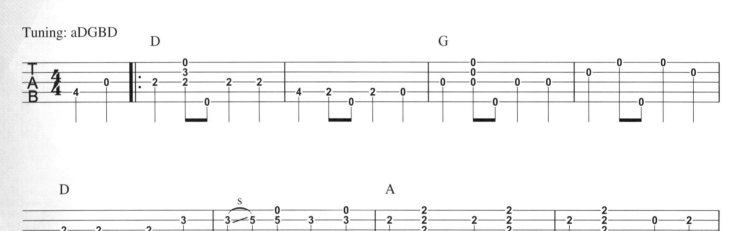

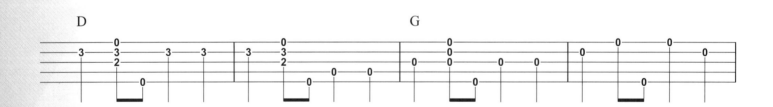

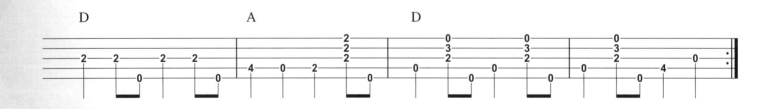

Wreck of the Old 97
(fancier melody)

Tuning: aDGBD

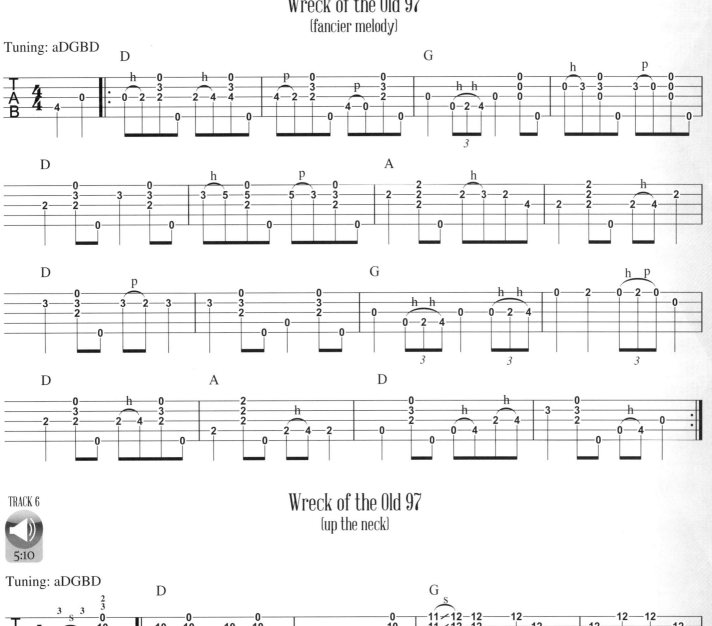

TRACK 6

5:10

Wreck of the Old 97
(up the neck)

Tuning: aDGBD

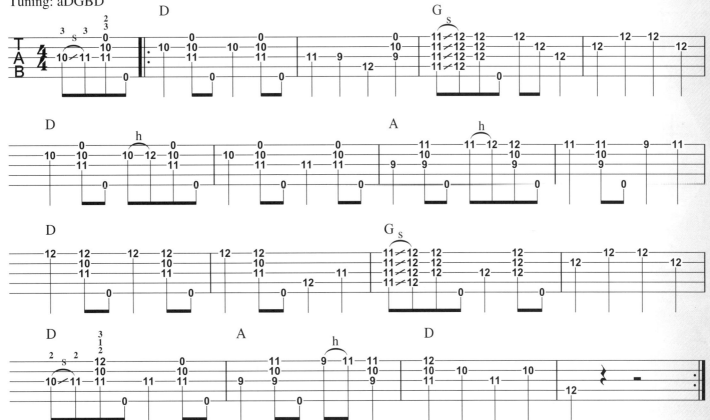

Soldier's Joy

"Soldier's Joy" is a great crossover tune that's played by old-time, bluegrass, and Celtic players. Most clawhammer players that I've met or heard like to play this tune in double-D tuning. Me, too! And at an old-time jam, I usually will. But at a bluegrass or Celtic jam, they like to change keys a lot—sometimes between every song, and sometimes even in the middle of a medley of tunes. So it's also useful to be able to play the tunes we like to play in double-D in open G tuning as well, and that's what we'll do here. Another thing about bluegrass jams is that you are expected to play a simple chord back-up while everyone else solos and then get fancy and play the melody when it's your turn to solo. So we'll do that here as well. To play tunes like this in D out of open G tuning, you'll want to tune or hook the fifth string up to A. Also, this tune is played with a shuffle feel.

Let's start out with a basic melody version of the tune.

TRACK 6

5:42

Soldier's Joy
(simple melody)

Tuning: aDGBD

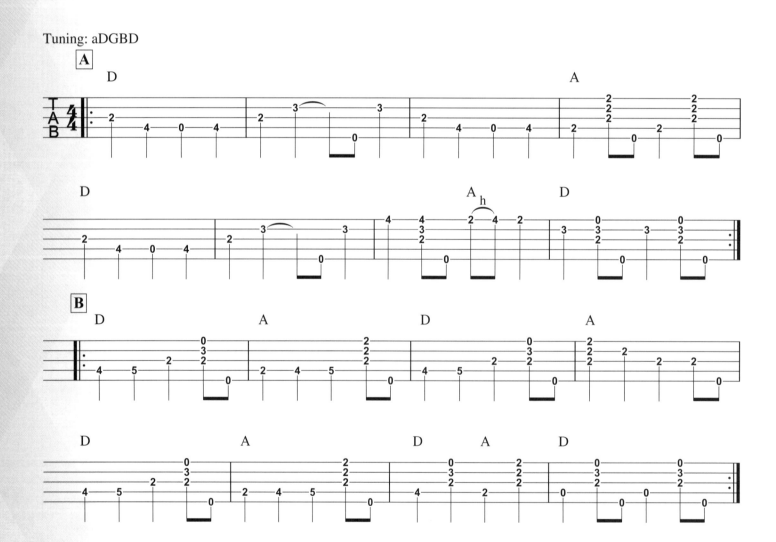

Now, here's a simple chord back-up that you can play at a bluegrass jam while others are soloing.

TRACK 6

6:15

Soldier's Joy
(chord back-up)

Tuning: aDGBD

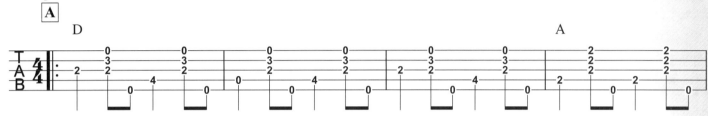

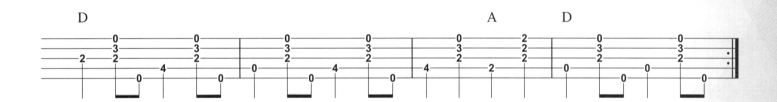

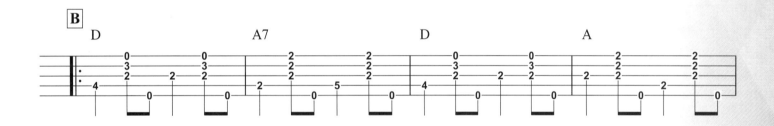

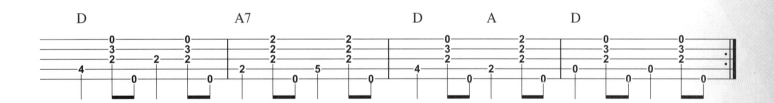

Here's another version that could be used as a solo but is really meant to show some possible ways you can play these chords with a melody in different places on the neck. It jumps around a lot, so have fun with it. There are no repeats shown here because both A parts and both B parts are different.

Soldier's Joy
(solo)

Tuning: aDGBD

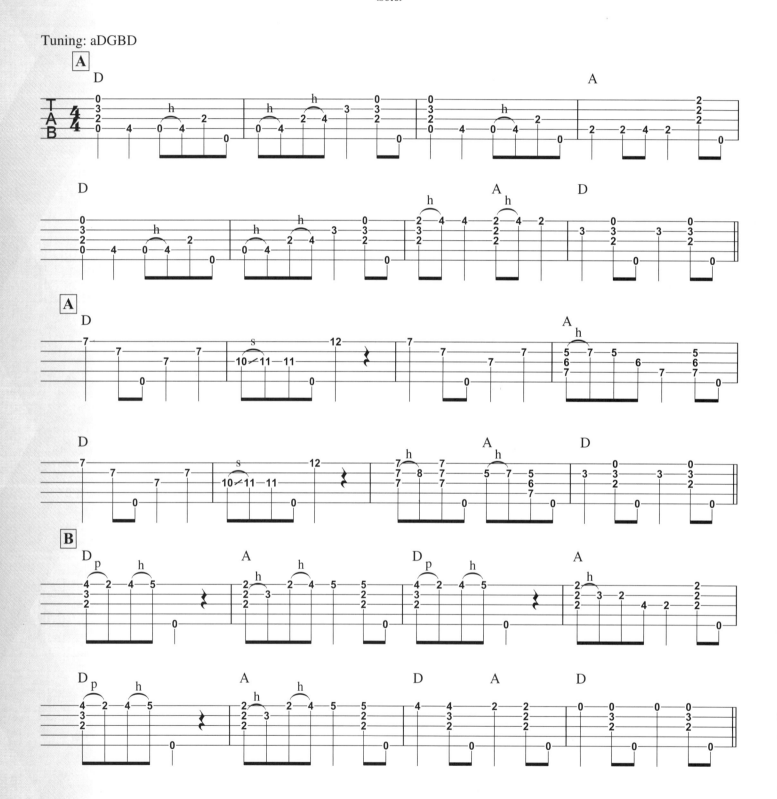

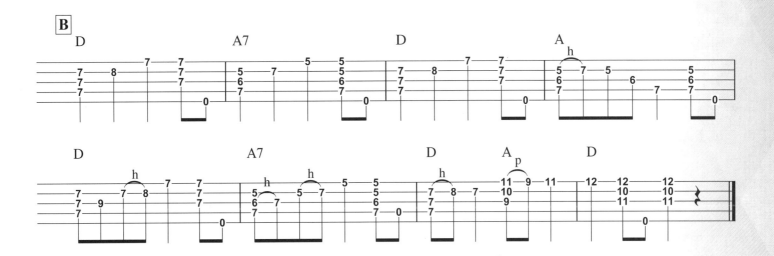

PLAYING IN THE KEY OF A

If you're in open G tuning and raise all five strings a whole step (two frets), you'll be in open A tuning. From there you can play any tune as if you were in G, but it'll be in the key of A because you raised every string by a whole step.

The good news is that if you can play in G, you can play in A. the I, IV, V, and all the other chords as well as the scales are exactly the same, but one whole step higher in pitch, because you move everything, including the open strings, up the neck by two frets.

We'll get to open A soon, but first, let's look at playing in the key of A from open G tuning. Why would anyone want to do this? There are no open strings for the A chord. Well, as I've said before, sometimes you just don't have the time to retune. Also, without a capo, you can play those notes that would normally lie behind the capo. So the D, E, and E7 chords (the IV, V, and V7 chords, respectively) will have open strings. Try this simple progression (be sure to tune the fifth string up to an A):

TRACK 7

0:00

Boil Them Cabbage Down
(in A from G tuning)

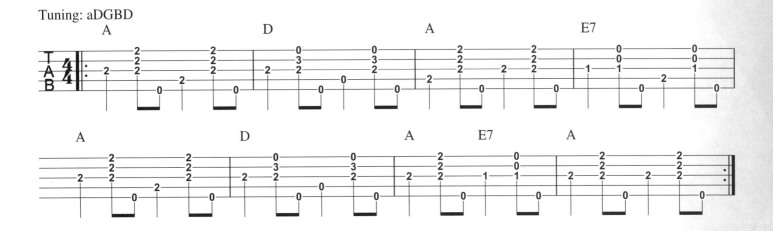

Now let's try "Make Me a Pallet," a song recorded by many, including Mississippi John Hurt (not on banjo, but it's a great version anyway). It's in the key of A but starts on the IV chord, D.

TRACK 7

🔊
0:17

Make Me a Pallet
(in A from G tuning)

Tuning: aDGBD

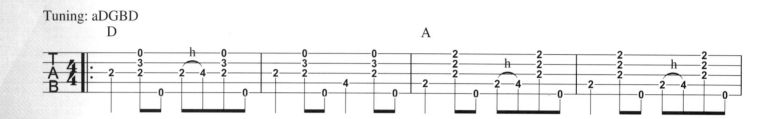

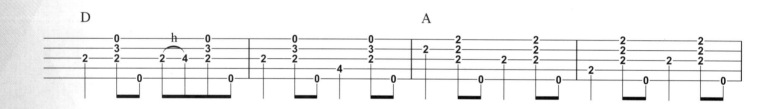

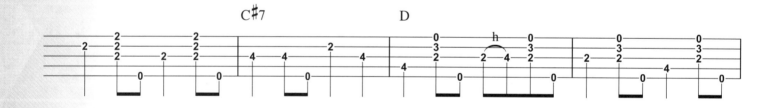

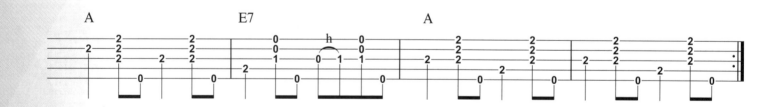

OPEN A TUNING

For open A tuning, you raise all five strings up a whole step (two frets). You can tune them up or put a capo on the second fret across the four long strings and also tune, hook, or otherwise raise the pitch of the fifth string by two frets. The strings are: a, E, A, C♯, and E. All of these tunes are played with a shuffle feel.

Sail Away Ladies

"Sail Away Ladies" is a great high-energy tune that works with or without words. If you play it as a fiddle tune, then it follows the standard AABB pattern. With some singers, it works better to just play ABAB. Play it however you like. Let's start with a simple melody.

TRACK 7

0:54

Sail Away Ladies
(melody)

Capo 2: aEAC♯E

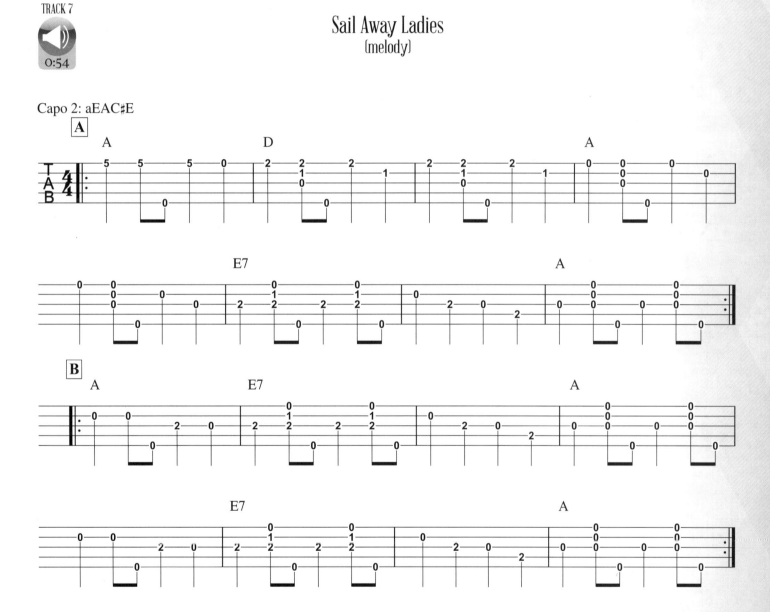

Sail Away Ladies
(chord back-up)

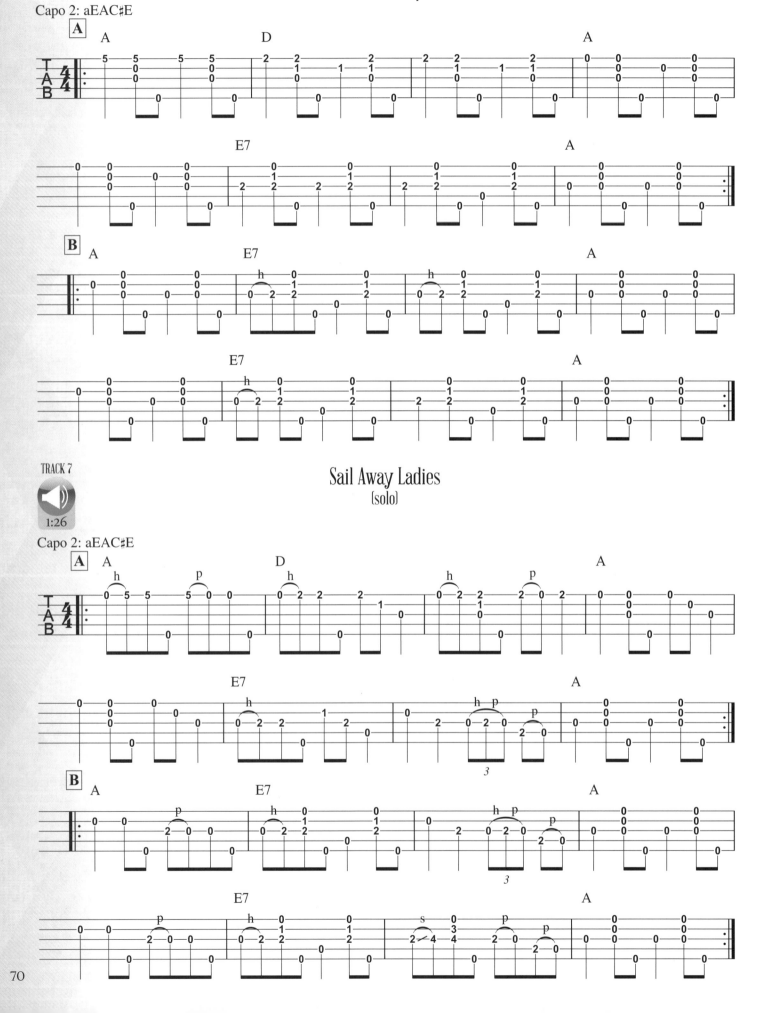

June Apple

"Sail Away Ladies" is in A major. "June Apple" and many other tunes, including "Old Joe Clark," which we looked at earlier, are in A Mixolydian. Mixolydian differs from the major scale in that the seventh note is flatted, or lowered by one half step (one fret). So A Mixolydian has a G instead of a G♯. In practical terms, this means melody notes on the first and fourth strings will be on the third fret above the capo instead of the fourth fret. Mixolydian tunes and songs often use the G major chord as well.

Here's the melody:

1:55

June Apple
(simple melody)

Capo 2: aEAC♯E

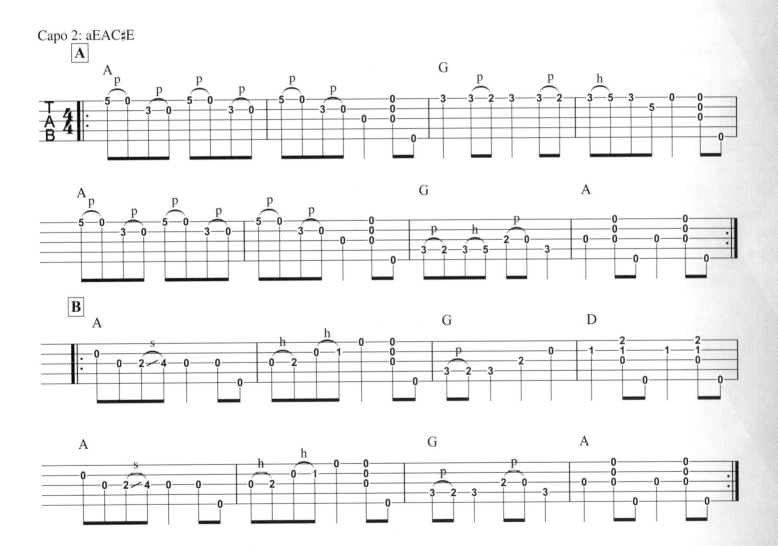

Now try a chord back-up:

TRACK 7

2:27

June Apple
(chord back-up)

Capo 2: aEAC#E

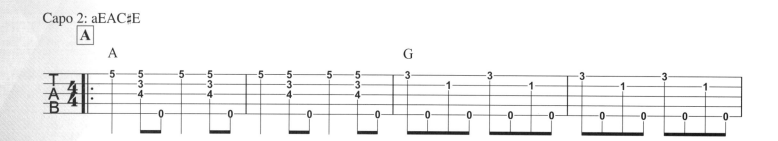

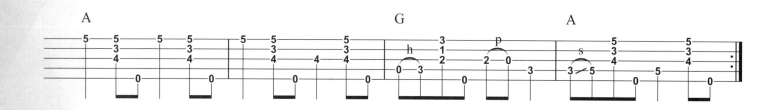

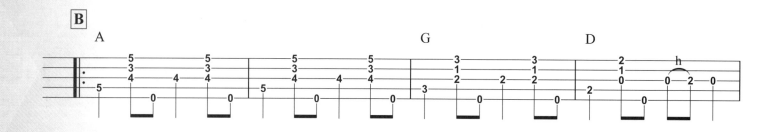

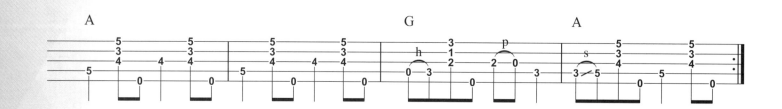

And here's an alternate melody version:

TRACK 7
3:01

June Apple
(alternate melody)

Capo 2: aEAC♯E

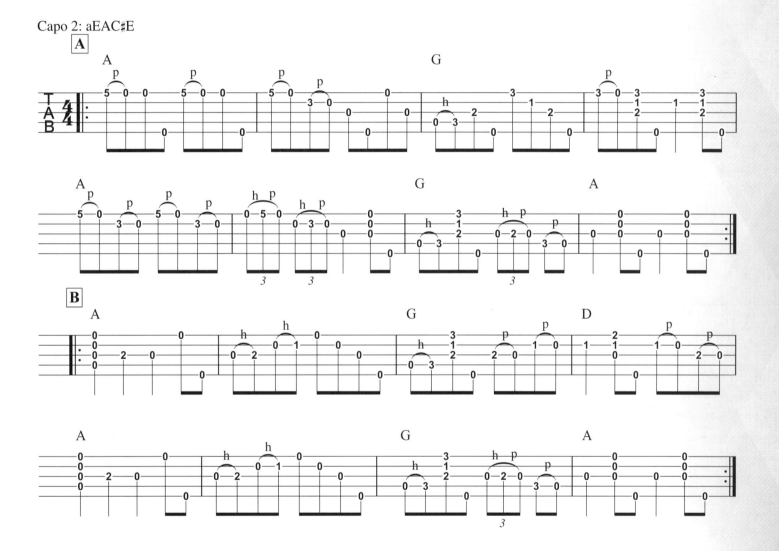

PLAYING OTHER KEYS (D, E, AND B) OUT OF OPEN A TUNING

Playing in the key of D out of open A tuning is just like playing in the key of C in open G tuning. You've just moved everything up the neck by one whole step (two frets). Go ahead and play "Dark Hollow" and "Will the Circle Be Unbroken" in D. Play them just like you did earlier, but they'll be up two frets because of the capo.

You can play in the key of E in this tuning just as you would play in the key of D in open G tuning. Play "Wreck of the Old 97" and "Soldier's Joy" in E.

And you can play in the key of B in open A tuning just as you would play the key of A in open G tuning. Play "Make Me a Pallet" in B.

★ CHAPTER 6 ★
TUNES A LA MODAL

One of the most common and most expressive banjo tunings is called "modal" (also known as "mountain modal," "mountain minor," or "sawmill"). Most clawhammer players that I've talked to or read about in my research prefer to approach modal tunes by playing the melody with some drone strings to fill out the sound and deepen the mood, rather than playing chords. That's generally how I like to play them as well. Then again, when playing with others, the guitars always seem to be able to play chords to these tunes. If they can do it, we can do it! So we'll look briefly at playing chords in this tuning, but we won't get carried away.

Most mountain modal tunes seem to be played in A when played with fiddles, but if there's no fiddle, we can play them in G or any key that suits us or suits the singer if it's a vocal song.

GETTING THERE

First, let's get into the tuning. It's just like open G tuning except the second string (B) is raised one half step (one fret) to C. So the notes are: g D G C D.

To use a tuner, just pluck the second string and turn the tuning peg to raise the pitch until you get to C. Or you can tune the second string up so that it matches the pitch of the third string at the fifth fret.

When you strum the open strings, you no longer have an open major chord—but it still sounds good. Technically, this is a Gsus4 chord; the 3rd (B) has been replaced by a 4th (C).

CHORDS FROM OPEN G SHAPES

Since this tuning is so close to open G (the second string is raised by one fret), you can play many of the chords you play in open G by just lowering any notes on the second string by one fret. So, for instance, to play an F chord, first finger it as you would in open G tuning and then lower the note on the second string by one fret. The same goes for the Dm chord, A chord, etc. Because an A chord shape is closed (fretted on all four strings), it's moveable up and down the neck to make any major chord.

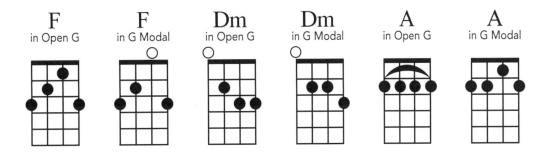

Some chords, such as an Em, are a little trickier; they have an open second string, and therefore you can't just lower it. In a case like this, you have many options. One is to not play the second string, which can be difficult if you want to strum or brush, but is doable when you play single notes. Another option is to go ahead and play it. The open C note on the second string turns an Em chord into and Em♭6, which may or may not sound good in the tune you're playing. Try it and see.

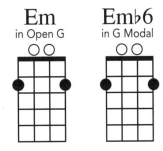

Now look at the E7 chord. You can't lower the second string, so you'll need to raise it to the next note in the chord, which is D, on the second fret.

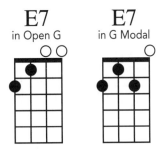

So, should you need a chord in this tuning, you can find it by starting with the chord shape from open G and then doing one of the following:
- Lower the note on the second string.
- Don't play the second string.
- Raise the note on the second string to the next note in the chord.

OTHER USEFUL CHORDS

A lot of G modal tunes only have two chords: G minor and F. Here's a good-sounding way to play a G minor in a modal song:

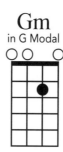

The notes of this chord, including the fifth string, are: g D G D D. The only notes are G and D: the root and 5th of the G minor chord—and the root and 5th of the G major chord! There's no 3rd, so this chord isn't really minor or major; yet it can be used for either. If you really want a full G minor sound, then add a finger on the third fret of the third string to add a ♭3rd (B♭). And, if for some reason you want it to really sound major, plop down a finger on the fourth fret of the third string.

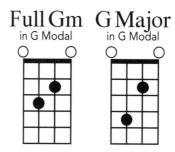

Here are more useful chords and variations that may come in handy. Playing the F and leaving the first string open adds a 6th to the chord, which usually sounds good. The D with no 3rd works as either a D major or D minor. The D7 is a great one-finger chord. The second C chord is the A major shape moved up the neck to fourth position. Note the B♭ chords. For the first one, you can leave either the first or fourth strings open if you like the sound or need a free finger. The last one has both the first and fourth strings open and looks suspiciously like a G minor.

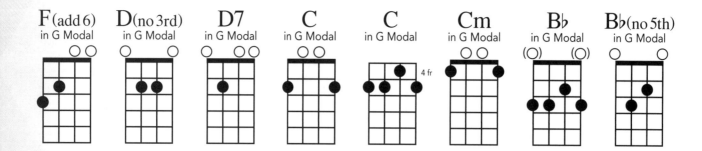

COLD RAIN AND SNOW

"Cold Rain and Snow" is in the Dorian mode (for those who care) and has been played by everyone from old-time to bluegrass to Celtic to the Grateful Dead to Pentangle (one of my favorites). I like to play it AAB (or verse–verse–chorus if it's sung), but feel free to double the B section if that's what you like. Here's a nice basic version.

TRACK 8

0:00

Cold Rain and Snow
(basic)

Tuning: gDGCD

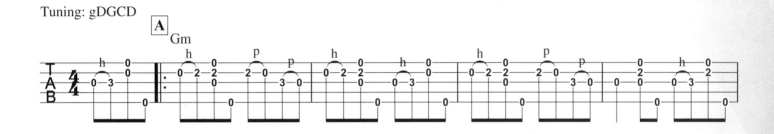

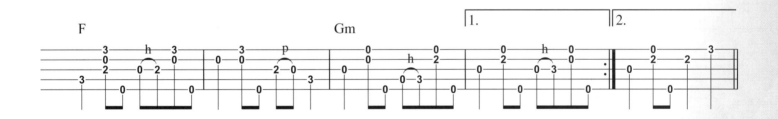

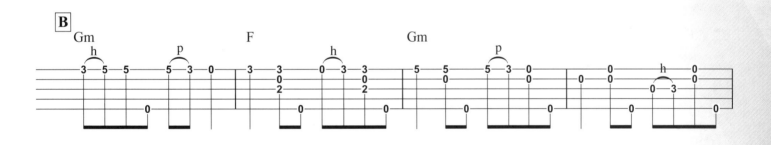

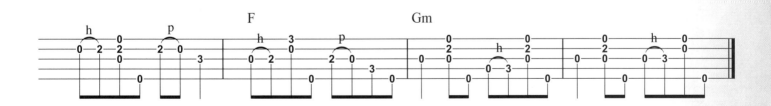

Here's a version that goes a little outside the box on the melody and up the neck a bit. Try it and see if you like it. I wrote out two variations for the A section.

0:52

Cold Rain and Snow
(variation)

Tuning: gDGCD

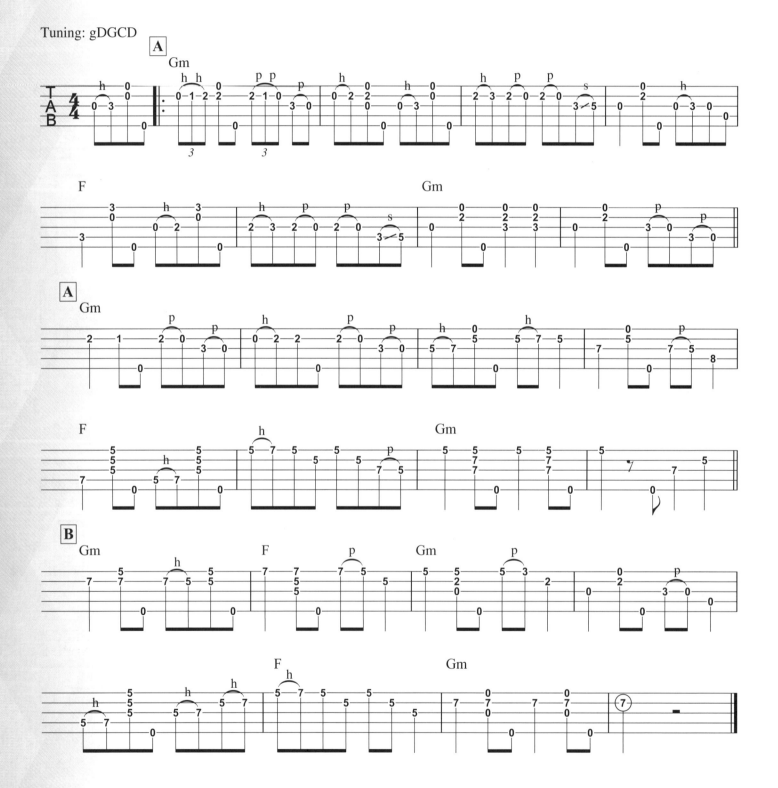

SHADY GROVE

"Shady Grove" is another tune that has stood the test of time. It began as the English folk ballad "Maddy Groves" in the 17th century. Today, it's a crossover tune played in many styles, with many variations in lyrics. Here's the basic melody.

TRACK 8

1:42

Shady Grove
(melody)

Tuning: gDGCD

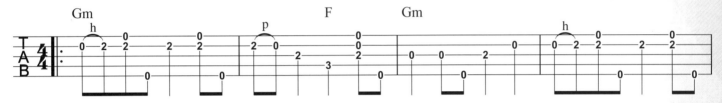

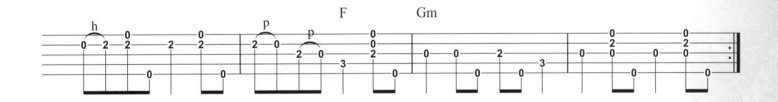

Here are some variations that show some of the things you can do when you play around in modal tuning. There are five variations covering much of the neck. The last one plays the melody in octaves—to play it you'll need a "double-claw" to play the first and fourth strings; I use my index and ring finger. Warning: don't be surprised if you get some funny looks if you play like this at a traditional jam!

TRACK 8

2:01

Shady Grove
(variations)

Tuning: gDGCD

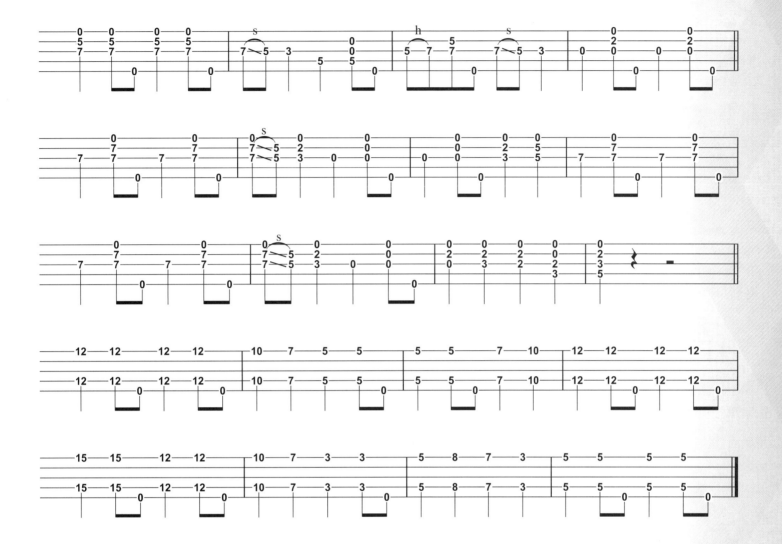

★ C H A P T E R 7 ★

DOUBLE PORTIONS

Double-C tuning (or double-D if you capo it up to the second fret) is a wonderful tuning used by most clawhammer players. Some use it as much or more than open G, because there are so many fiddle tunes in the key of D.

While it's very useful to be able to play D tunes out of open G tuning for the sake of being able to switch keys without retuning on stage or at a jam, double-C/double-D has a great traditional sound and lends itself well to playing melodies. This tuning also works well for playing in C or D minor; we'll look at that a little.

GETTING THERE

Double-C tuning is: g C G C D. To get there, raise the second string from B to C (as you do for G modal tuning) and also lower the fourth string one whole step (two frets) to C. If you don't have or don't like using tuners, then raise the second string until it's the same pitch as the fifth fret of the third string to make it a C. Then, using the second string as a reference, lower the fourth string until it's an octave below the second string. Alternately, you can fret the fourth string at the seventh fret and lower it until it's the same pitch as the open third string.

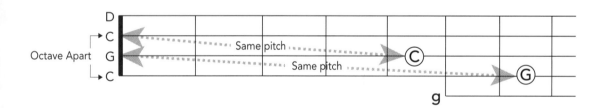

To get to double-D, capo the four long strings on the second fret and hook, tune, or otherwise raise the fifth string one whole step (two frets) to A, so you have: a D A D E.

BASIC CHORDS

To play about a million tunes in double-C/double-D, you only need three chords: the I, IV, and V. In double-C, that's C, F, and G; in double-D, that's D, G, and A. Here they are:

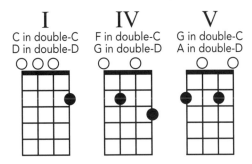

If these are new to you, then play "Boil Them Cabbage Down" in this tuning a few times to get a feel for them. This one is played with a shuffle feel.

TRACK 9

0:00

Boil Them Cabbage Down
(double-C/double-D)

Tuning: gCGCD
(or capo II: aDADE)

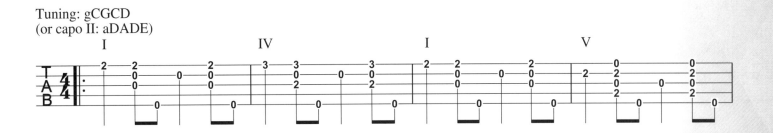

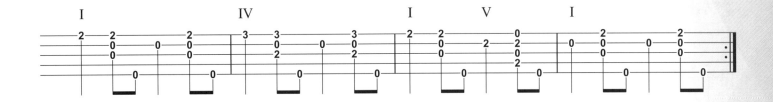

BASIC MELODIES

Double-C/double-D is great for playing melodies. Here's a two-octave scale to help you get the feel for where the melody notes are.

TRACK 9

0:19

Scale Exercise 1

Tuning: gCGCD
(or capo II: aDADE)

Here it is again with a little bit o' the claw.

TRACK 9

0:36

Scale Exercise 2

Tuning: gCGCD
(or capo II: aDADE)

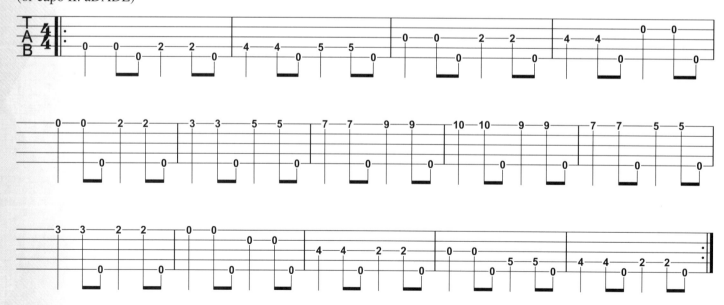

FLY AROUND MY PRETTY LITTLE MISS (SUSANNAH GAL)

This tune, known by many names, is really fun to play. Here's a melody-only version using the notes from the previous scale exercise. Since this one is usually played in D, it is also presented here in D; it's also played with a shuffle feel.

TRACK 9

1:05

Fly Around My Pretty Little Miss

Tuning: Double-C, capo II (aDADE)

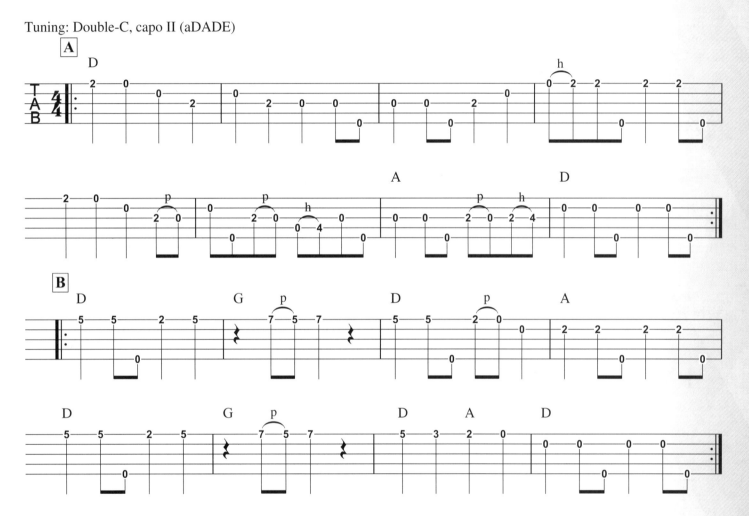

MORE CHORDS

Here are a few additional chords that you may run across as you learn tunes and songs in this tuning.

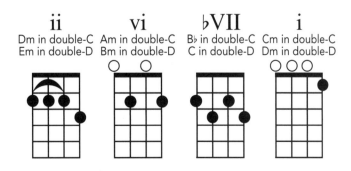

ii	vi	♭VII	i
Dm in double-C	Am in double-C	B♭ in double-C	Cm in double-C
Em in double-D	Bm in double-D	C in double-D	Dm in double-D

MIDNIGHT ON THE WATER

"Midnight on the Water" is a shuffled waltz that uses both the ii minor and vi minor chords. This one is also usually played in D, but feel free to play it in C (or any other key your heart desires).

TRACK 9

1:37

Midnight on the Water

Tuning: Double-C, capo II (aDADE)

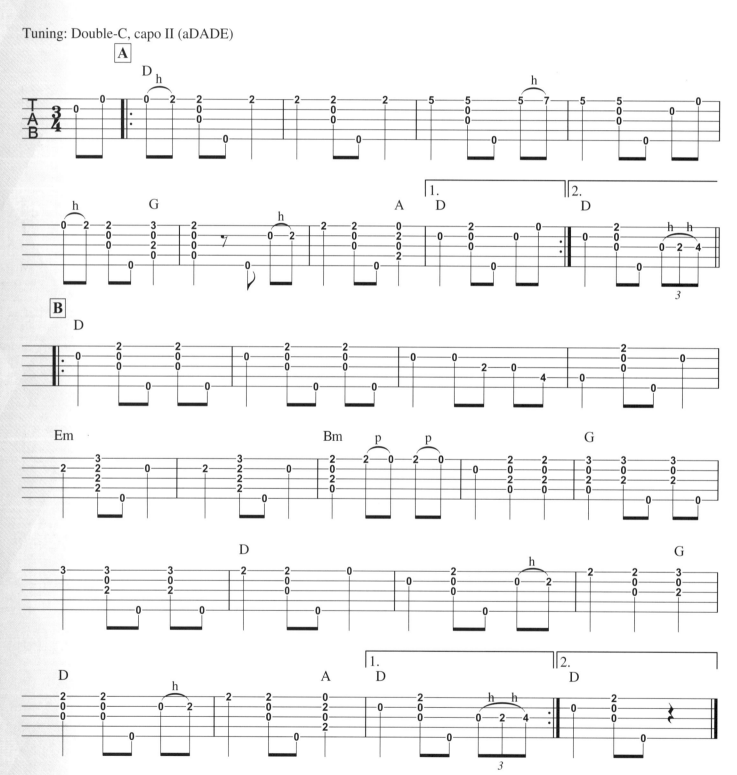

HOME WITH THE GIRLS IN THE MORNING

"Home with the Girls in the Morning" is a haunting minor modal tune that uses the i minor chord (Cm in double-C, Dm in double-D) and the major ♭VII chord (B♭ in double-C and C in double-D). Again, this one has the chords for the key of D. First, here's a basic melody. It follows the standard AABB pattern, but the second time through the B part, one of the D minor chords is changed to a D major—a very dramatic and unexpected sound.

TRACK 9

2:27

Home with the Girls in the Morning
(melody)

Tuning: Double-C, capo II (aDADE)

Here's another version with more variation.

Home with the Girls in the Morning
(variation)

Tuning: Double-C, capo II (aDADE)

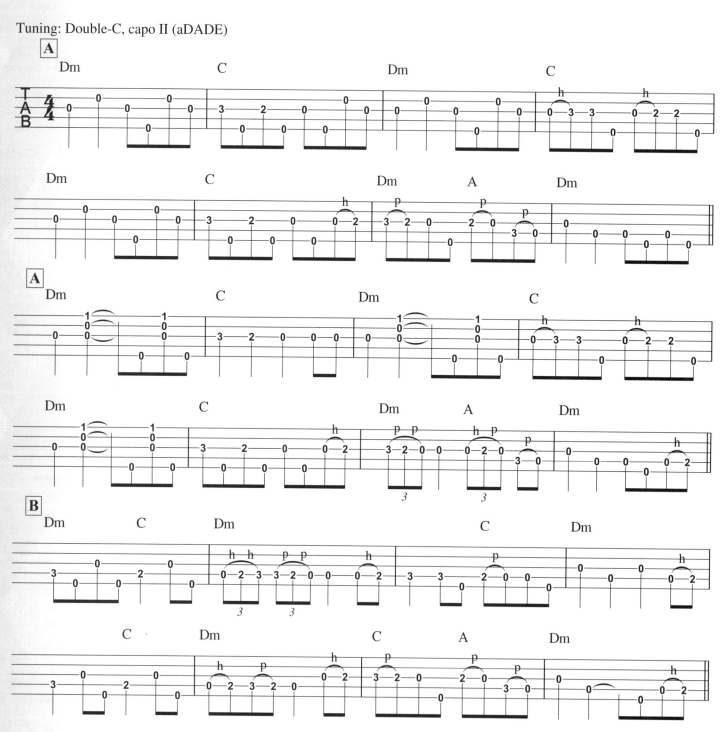

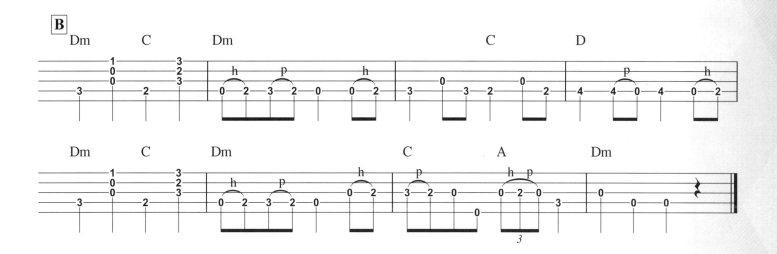

PLAYING CHORDS UP THE NECK

Here are some additional ways to play the I, IV, and V chords up the neck. The fret markings (numbers to the right) indicate above the nut if you're playing in double-C and above the capo if you're playing in another key.

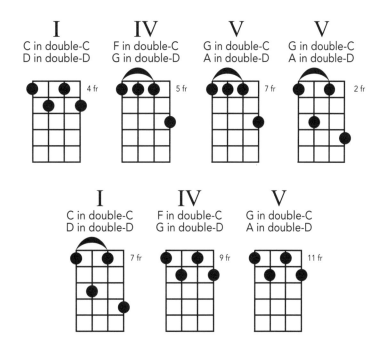

COLEMAN'S MARCH

"Coleman's March" has become a standard at our local jams because of the beautiful melody and interesting chord progression. It sounds good fast or slow and lends itself well to playing up the banjo neck. It's played AABB, and I wrote out separate versions for each A and B section, with each presented in two octaves.

TRACK 9

4:26

Coleman's March
(melody in two octaves)

Tuning: Double-C, capo II (aDADE)

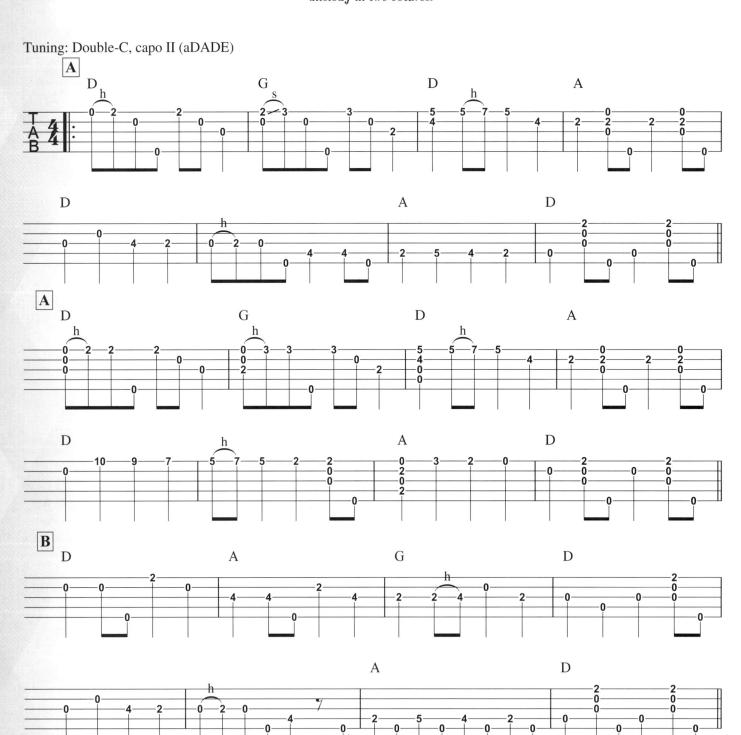

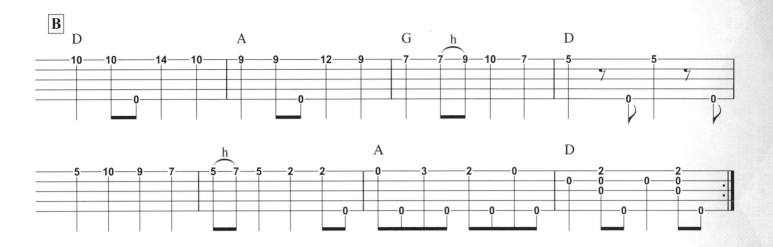

Here's another version with more chords and partial chords.

Coleman's March
(chord version)

Tuning: Double-C, capo II (aDADE)

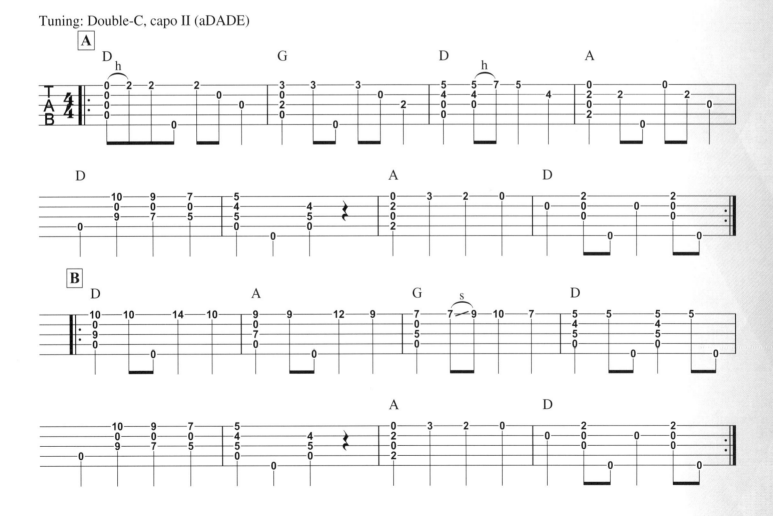

★ CHAPTER 8 ★
CHORD ON BLUES

Banjo has been a part of country blues for a long time, and there's even a well-known song called "Country Blues" by Doc Boggs. Blues has become a near universal musical form. In simplest terms, it's a chord progression that follows this, or a variation of, this pattern (one four-beat measure per chord):

I   I   I   I

IV   IV   I   I

V   IV   I   I

There are many variations on the pattern, ranging from eight to 12 bars, and even beyond. In practice, there's a lot more to it—far more than can be covered in a short chapter. But we'll do what we can. Blues tends to have a lot of seventh chords—often all seventh chords: I7, IV7, and V7.

There are so many different types of blues tunes with different rhythms and feels that it could fill a whole cookbook. Since I need to leave room for a lot of other stuff, you get two: a (possibly) familiar song and an instrumental I made up just for the fun of it.

DEEP ELUM BLUES

"Deep Elum Blues" is a song with many versions played by many people in many styles. It lends itself well to a bouncy banjo feel. Every version I've heard uses a different amount of measures, and they all have their charm. Here, it's in a straight 12-bar blues format—except that I wrote it as 24 bars to make the notes easier to read. Play it with a shuffle feel.

We'll play this one in double-D tuning, starting with a version that brings out the melody.

TRACK 10

0:00

Deep Elum Blues
(melody)

Tuning: Double-C, capo II (aDADE)

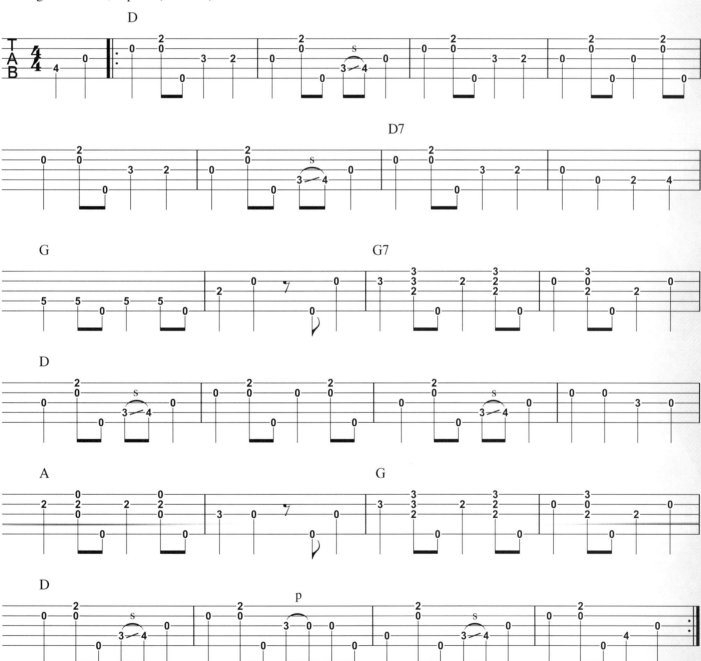

In a blues jam, as in a bluegrass jam, most of the people play a rhythm back-up while anyone can take a solo. Rhythm back-ups can be very basic, but they don't have to be boring. Here's one that uses a typical blues pattern that echoes the melody without interfering with soloists. Keep it bouncy, and watch for the pinky stretches in the A and G chords.

TRACK 10

0:48

Deep Elum Blues
(chord back-up)

Tuning: Double-C, capo II (aDADE)

So you're jamming away on "Deep Elum Blues" with a bunch of people, and someone looks at you and says, "Take it!" What do you do? Actually... almost anything. You could play the melody. You could claw a simple version of the chords with some extra hammer-ons and pull-offs. You could bang out a rhythm on the banjo head. That's one of the great things about blues; it's wide open! Plus, since banjo may be new to most blues jams, anything you do will sound new and different (and hopefully, good, too). Here's one way to take a clawhammer solo on this song—just one way. Have some fun, experiment, and come up with your own solo.

TRACK 10

1:35

Deep Elum Blues
(solo)

Tuning: Double-C, capo II (aDADE)

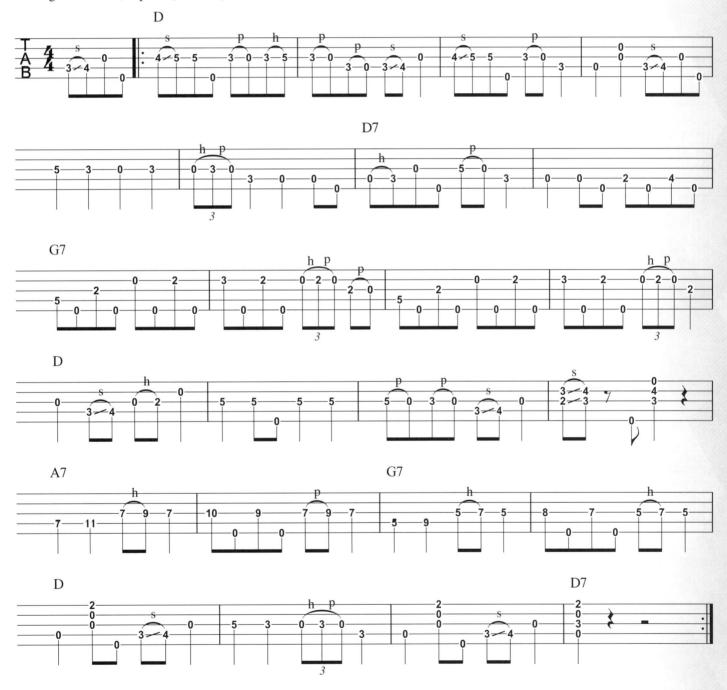

GENERIC BLUES IN G

Here's a slow 12-bar blues in G just for the fun of it. Notice the classic descending turnaround licks in the intro and the 11th and 12th bars. It has a shuffle rhythm, so each beat of each 4/4 measure feels like a triplet. There are two variations.

TRACK 10

2:22

Generic Blues in G

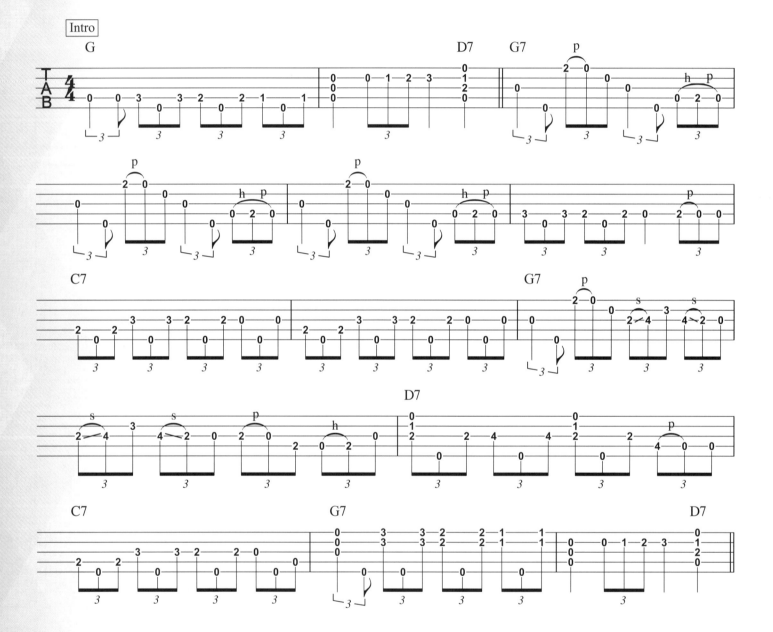

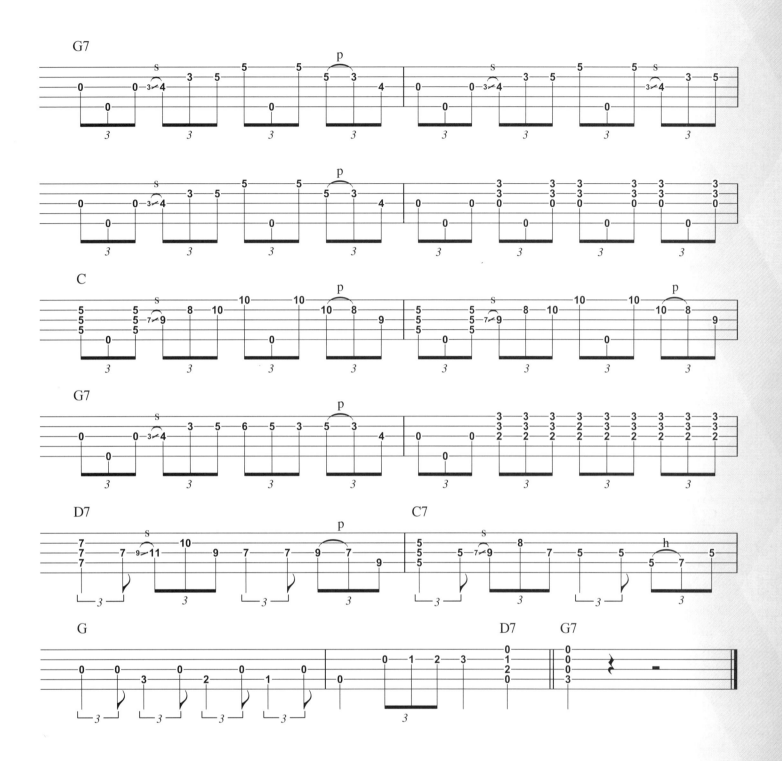

Blues is a big musical world that, in my opinion, needs more banjo. Anyone else think so?

★ CHAPTER 9 ★
HOLIDAY DELIGHTS

It's that special time of the year when we all believe there's a chance for peace on Earth and hold in our hearts goodwill to all men and women. The family is gathered together under one roof. Multiple generations are working together in the kitchen to prepare a feast of favorite foods. Nothing could make this day any better—except, of course, some banjo.

Whether you supply live background music or get the whole family to sing along, being able to play a few of the traditional tunes of the season adds a personal touch to a family holiday. (And by playing for family after dinner, it's a good way to get out of washing about a million dishes, pots, and pans.)

If your family sings a lot and knows the songs, then giving a count, maybe a short intro, and playing simple chords is all you'll need for a good sing-along. If your family doesn't regularly sing, then you may want to help out by keeping the melody going.

I can't supply the whole holiday repertoire here, but I can give you a sampling that should help you get started and give you some ideas on how to approach the songs.

GOD REST YE MERRY GENTLEMEN

"God Rest Ye Merry Gentlemen" is a nice minor melody with some interesting chord possibilities. Here's a way to play it that's mostly melody with just a little hint of chord now and then. Maybe play it once through and then revert to simpler chords when people start singing.

TRACK 11

0:00

God Rest Ye Merry Gentlemen

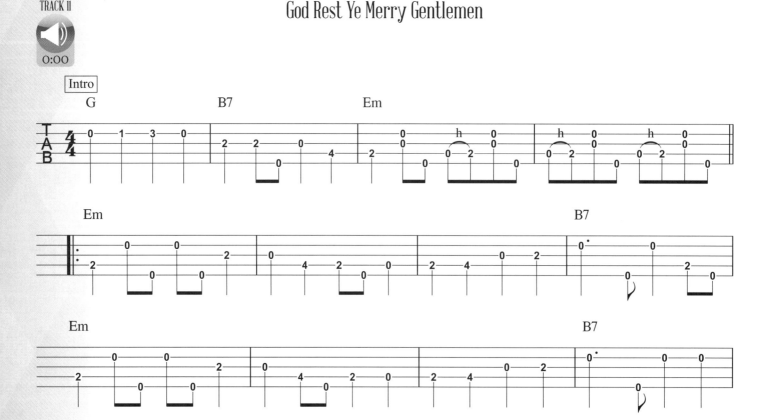

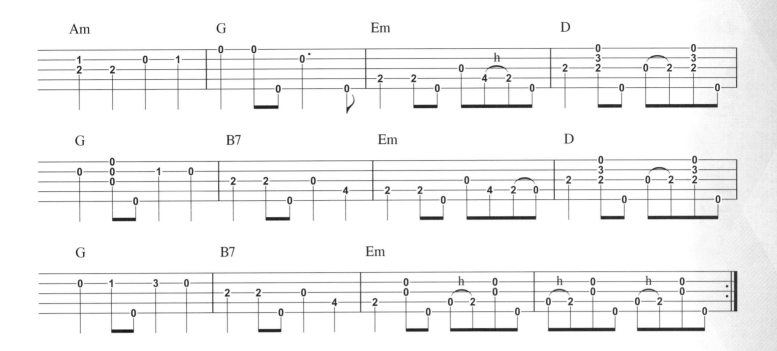

DREIDEL, DREIDEL, DREIDEL

This is a children's Hanukkah song that feels to me like a simple fiddle tune. Try it in AABB format, speed it up, and have fun with it.

TRACK 11
0:46

Dreidel, Dreidel, Dreidel
(simple)

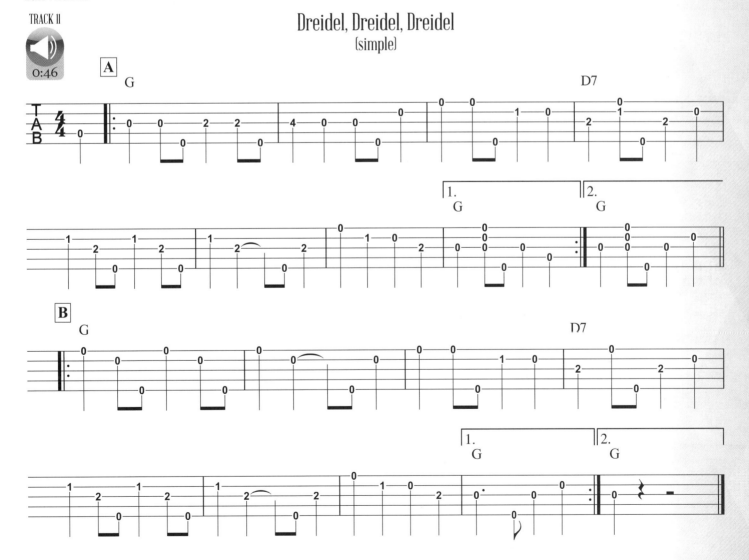

Here it is again as an example of how you can improvise around a simple melody to make it more fun to play.

TRACK II

1:16

Dreidel, Dreidel, Dreidel
(fun)

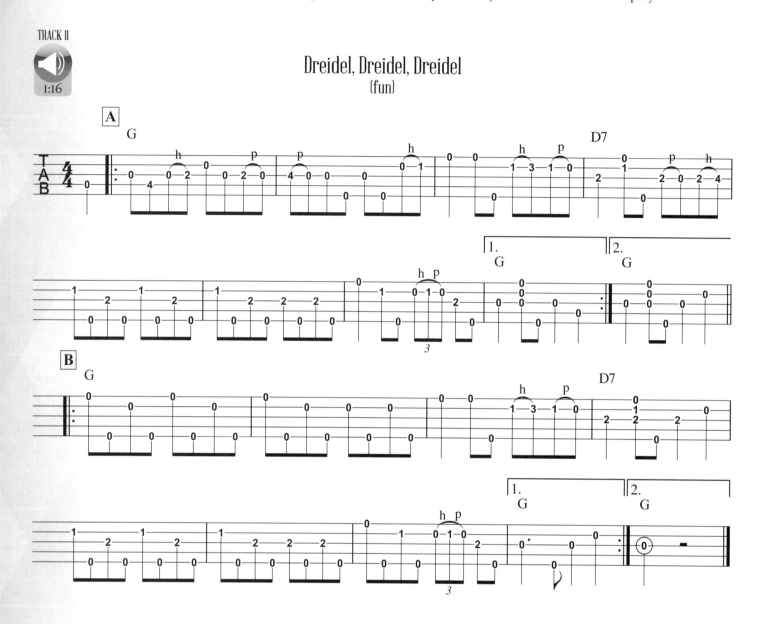

DECK THE HALLS

Next is a cheerful old favorite most people are familiar with. The first version is a nice, bouncy melody. We'll play it in double-C tuning.

Deck the Halls
(melody)

Tuning: gCGCD

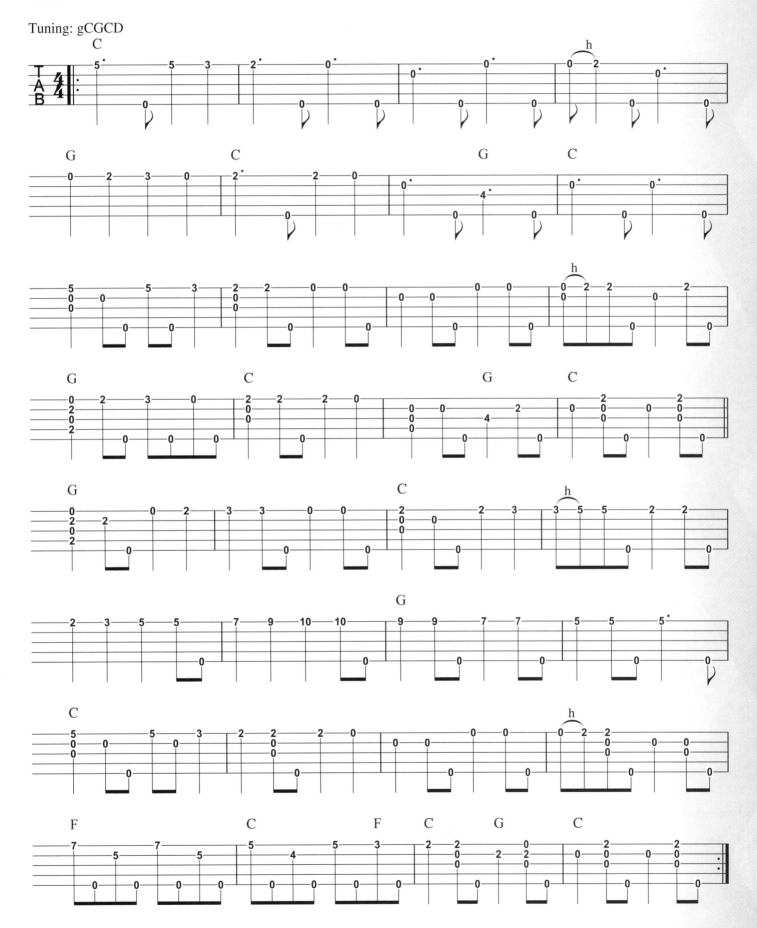

Here's a statelier version with lots of chord fragments up the neck.

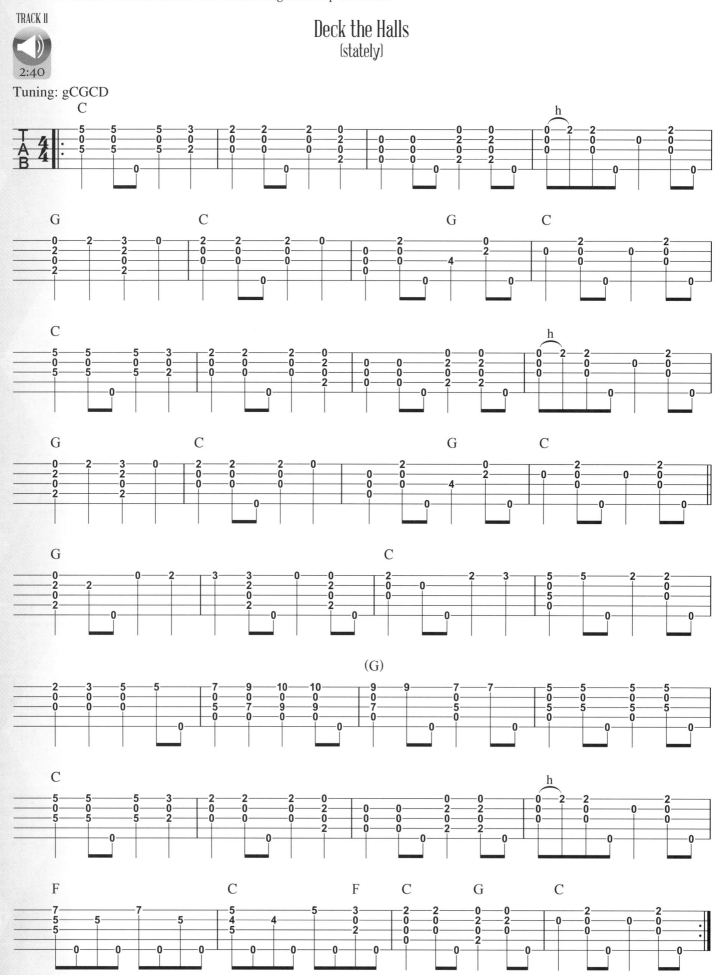

Deck the Halls
(stately)

Tuning: gCGCD

AULD LANG SYNE

Happy New Year! This one's also in double-C.

TRACK 11

3:25

Tuning: gCGCD

Auld Lang Syne

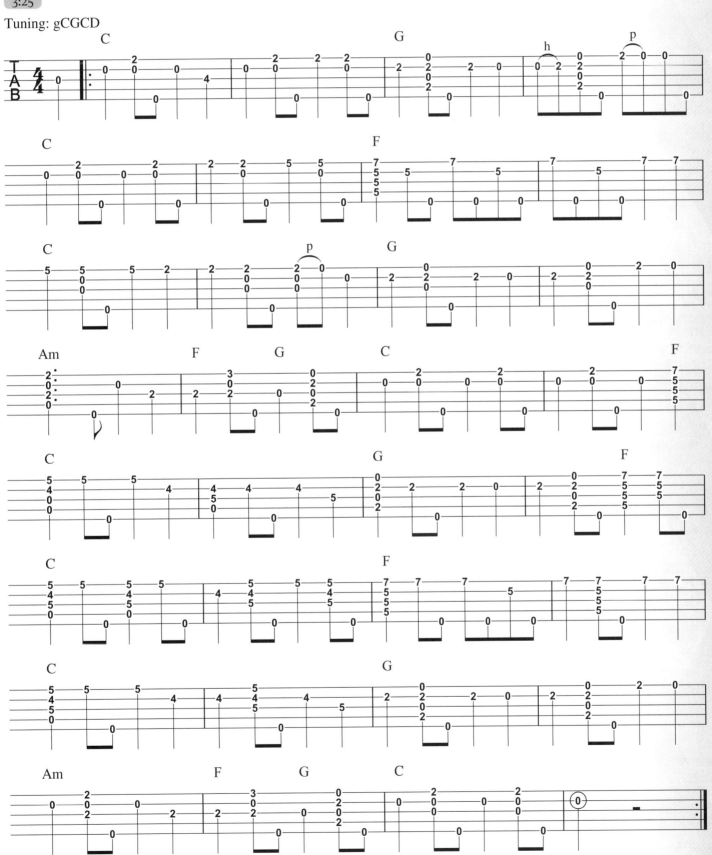

CHAPTER 10

FOR THE KIDS

Kids need music, too, and the boisterous, bouncy banjo is a great way to serve it to them. Children's songs are the hot dogs and mac 'n' cheese of the music world. You don't really need a cookbook to whip up these simple dishes, but it's nice to have them listed and included as a reminder of our youth and how much we enjoyed them.

You'll probably want to keep the arrangements simple when playing them for children. Keep the melody very clear (not too syncopated), especially when they're singing, but you can fancy it up during a verse when the kids are dancing or clapping.

Beyond entertaining kids and helping them to establish a love of music, these songs can be excellent learning tools for us as developing musicians. We know the melodies to these tunes, and they're usually not too complicated, so figuring them out on the banjo is a great way to develop the ear and the ability to play things you've never played before.

Here are a few of my favorites.

ROW, ROW, ROW YOUR BOAT

"Row, Row, Row Your Boat" is the classic round that everyone I know sang as a child. The first version is a very simple, mostly brushing, arrangement that really shows the melody and would be good for getting the kids started or teaching the song. The second version is more fun to play and will work with kids once they know the song, but be sure to clearly accent the melody notes. We'll play it in open G tuning here for simplicity, but capo up to any key that works for your kids (C and D are often good keys for kids).

TRACK 12

0:00

Row, Row, Row Your Boat

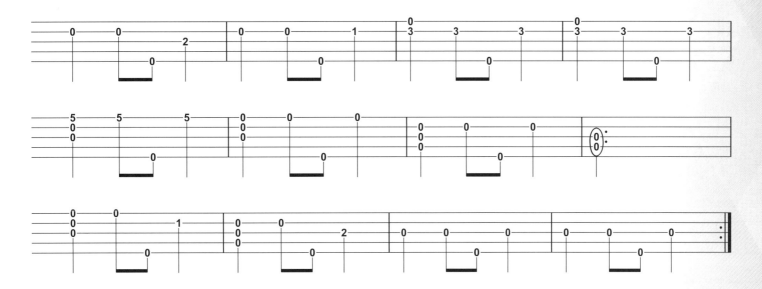

This song also lends itself well to alternate verses, which can help keep the kids' interest and inspire some giggles or screams. For instance, replace the second two lines with, "If you see an alligator, don't forget to scream." Then let them all scream!

ARE YOU SLEEPING?

Another classic from my childhood, this one is ever more appropriate for today's multicultural world, since it's sung in many languages and can be used to include, share, and learn about everyone and their backgrounds. As a child, it was my first exposure to French, and I also learned it in Hebrew. A simple web search will bring you lyrics in many languages, including French (of course), Spanish, Hebrew, Swahili, Albanian, Chinese, Czech, and at least a dozen more. You can substitute harmonics at the 12th fret in the last two or four measures to get a bell ringing sound. Again, it is shown in open G tuning.

TRACK 12

0:41

Are You Sleeping?

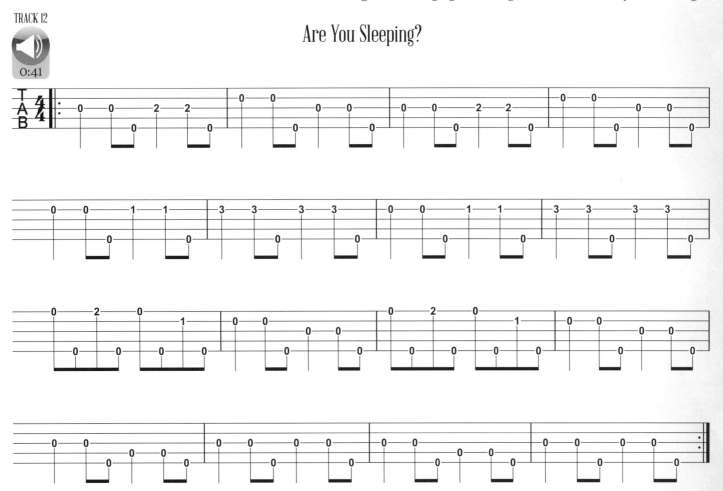

OLD MACDONALD

"Old MacDonald" is a very fun song for kids (and some of us not overly mature adults) because we—I mean they—get to make animal sounds. And it never hurts to add in a few "cha-cha-chas" either. I guess Mr. MacDonald was a good farmer, even if he didn't know how to spell farm.

TRACK 12

1:13

Old MacDonald

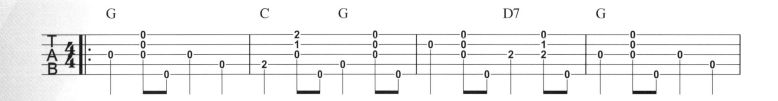

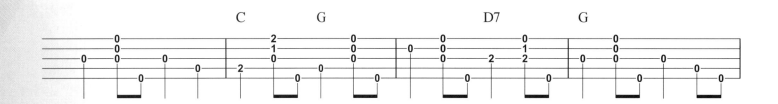

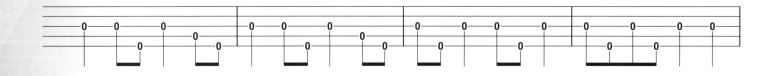

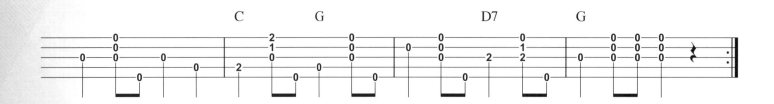

TWINKLE, TWINKLE LITTLE STAR

Here's a nice, slow lullaby for kids to sing or for you to play as they settle down for a nap. It works out very nicely in two octaves in double-D tuning. This first version is simple—mostly chord brushes with the melody outlined—and is good to sing with.

TRACK 12

1:44

Twinkle, Twinkle Little Star
(simple)

Tuning: Double-C, capo II (aDADE)

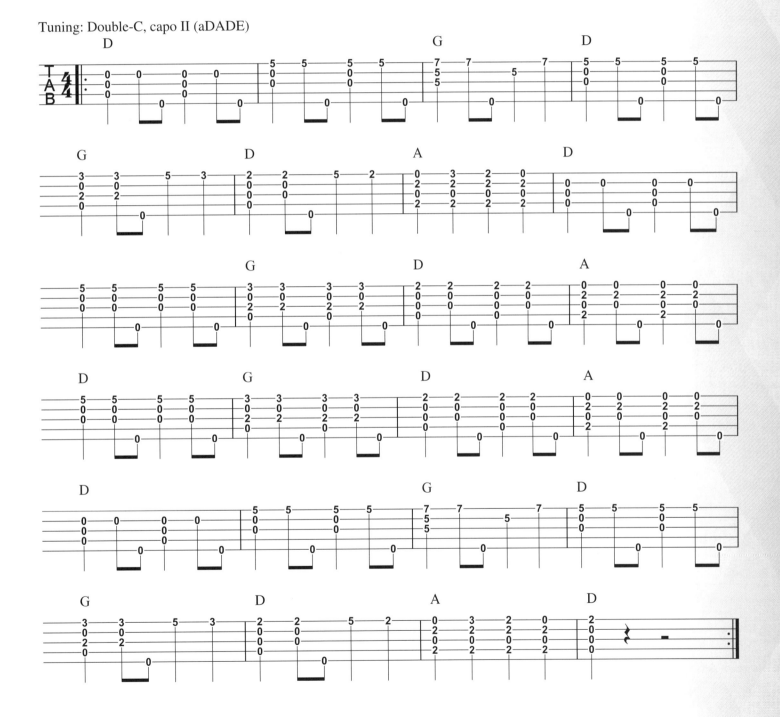

Here's a version that lets you have some fun with the melody. It's more for quiet listening time than for accompanying the kids.

2:35

Twinkle, Twinkle Little Star
(melodic)

Tuning: Double-C, capo II (aDADE)

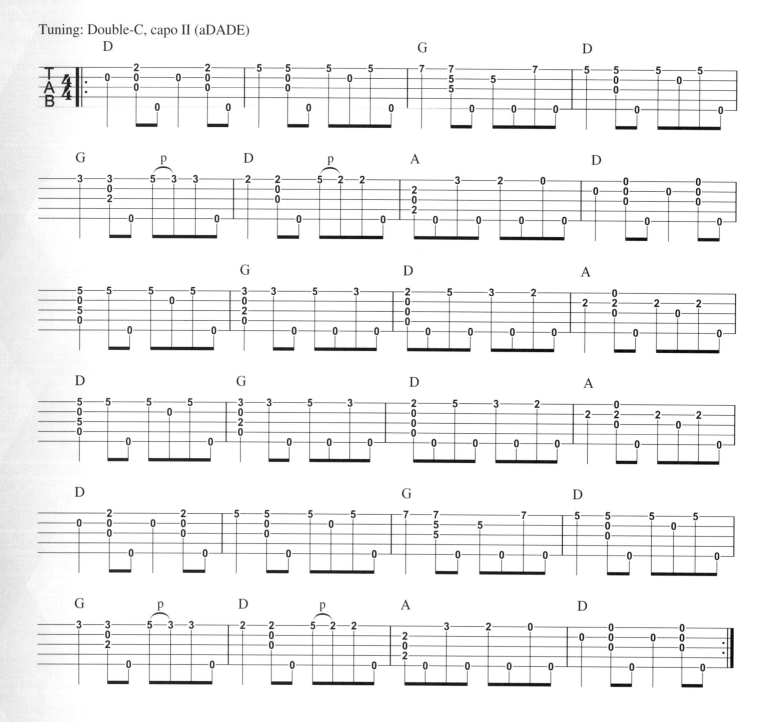

Here's one more version, in the lower octave—because it's there.

TRACK 12

3:27

Twinkle, Twinkle Little Star
(lower octave)

Tuning: Double-C, capo II (aDADE)

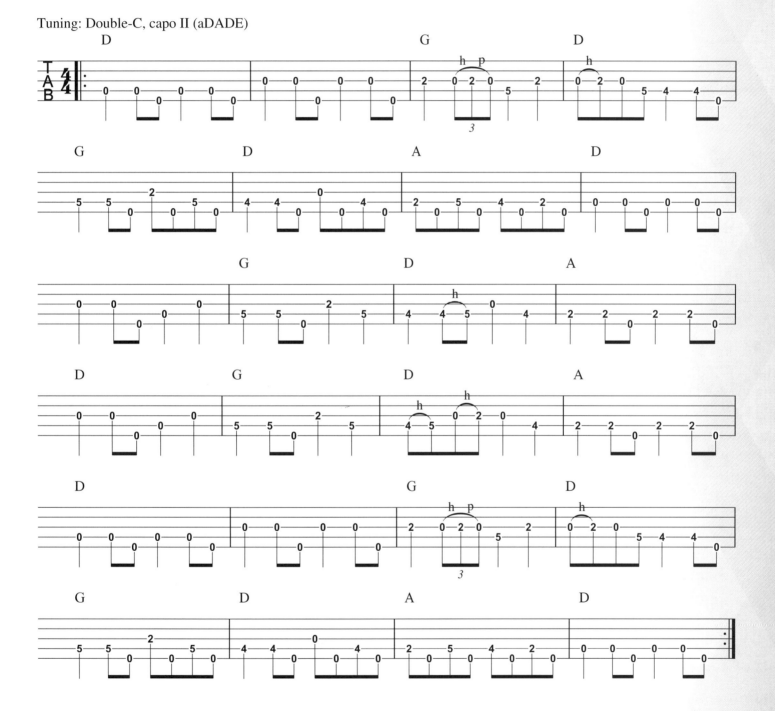

★ CHAPTER 11 ★
THE CLASSICS

For centuries, composers have taken simple but beautiful folk melodies and turned them into symphonies and other orchestral pieces. I think it's time we did some taking back. Here are a few simple melodies stolen—er... adapted—from orchestral works and turned into fiddle tune-like banjo pieces.

ODE TO JOY

"Ode to Joy" is from the final movement of Beethoven's ninth symphony and is usually heard with full orchestra and choir. But taken down to a simple melody, it becomes a pretty little tune that is open to all sorts of improvisation and variation. It's very short and makes a nice piece if you play it many times through, starting very simply and getting a little fancier each time. This is another thing that we can "borrow" from the composers: *theme and variations*. First play the theme (or melody) and then play it again and again, each time in a slightly different way. I've supplied a few variations here, but don't settle for what I've given you—add your favorite touches and techniques to this tune and make it your own.

TRACK 13

0:00

Ode to Joy
(variation 1)

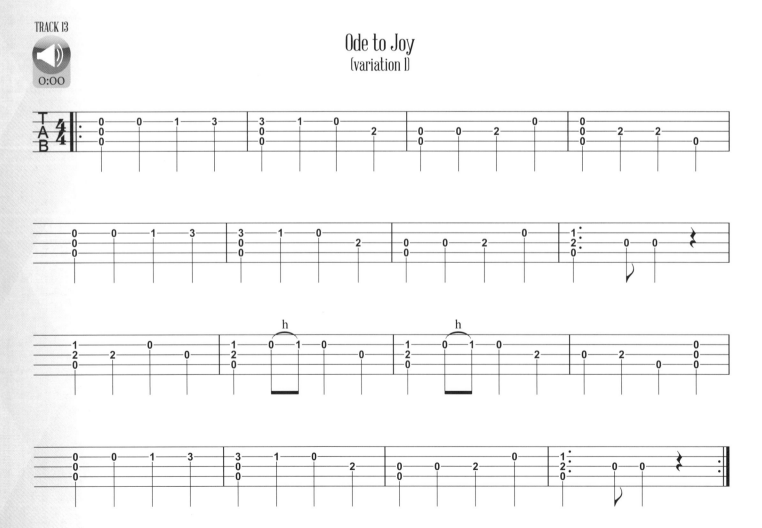

TRACK 13

0:37

Ode to Joy
(variation 2)

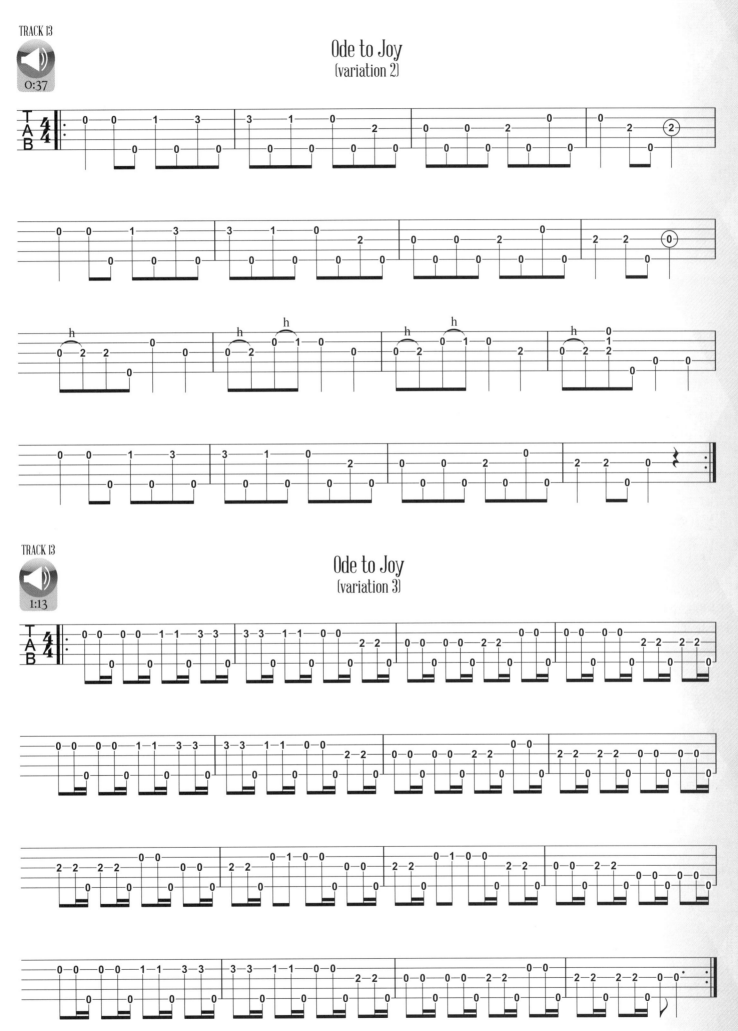

TRACK 13

1:13

Ode to Joy
(variation 3)

TRACK 13

1:51

Ode to Joy
(variation 4)

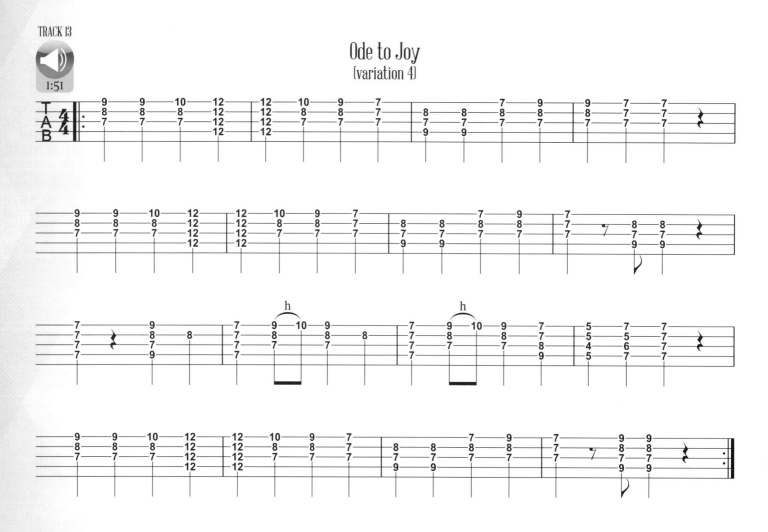

WILLIAM TELL OVERTURE

This one is familiar to fans of the old Western TV (and radio) show. It was taken from Rossini's William Tell opera. Some may think that Rossini may have objected to the use of his composition for the theme song of a cowboy show, but I'm sure he'd wholeheartedly approve of this banjo version. I've been playing it for years, and he hasn't complained yet.

This is a very much simplified version, and even the intro has been shortened. As shown here, it has this form:

Intro A A B B C C A

But feel free to extend it in any way that sounds good to you. Also, this is a simple version of the melody; have some fun with it.

TRACK 13

2:35

William Tell Overture

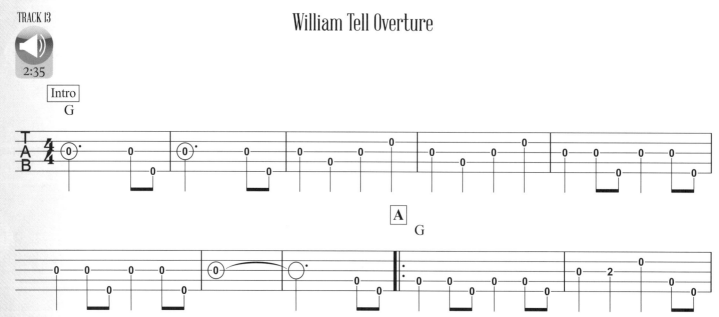

CANON IN D MAJOR

Commonly known as "Pachelbel's Canon" (because it was written by the German Baroque composer Johann Pachelbel), this piece is familiar to many people and finds its way into many weddings. The interesting thing about it is that it doesn't have a catchy melody—in fact, there's not much of a melody at all. What we react to (and remember) is the chord progression.

So, to play a banjofied version of the canon, just play the chords over and over in different ways. I guarantee that if you play this at a wedding, everyone will recognize it, and nobody (except the brother-in-law who plays violin—not fiddle—with the local philharmonic) will appreciate it. Classic style picking allows a lot more options for playing fancy arpeggios, but we clawhammerers can still plunk out some pretty chordage.

Here's four times through the progression. Take it slow and stately. For the first couple of variations, really bring out the first note of each measure to establish the piece and then take liberties. And add your own variations.

TRACK 13

3:48

Canon in D Major

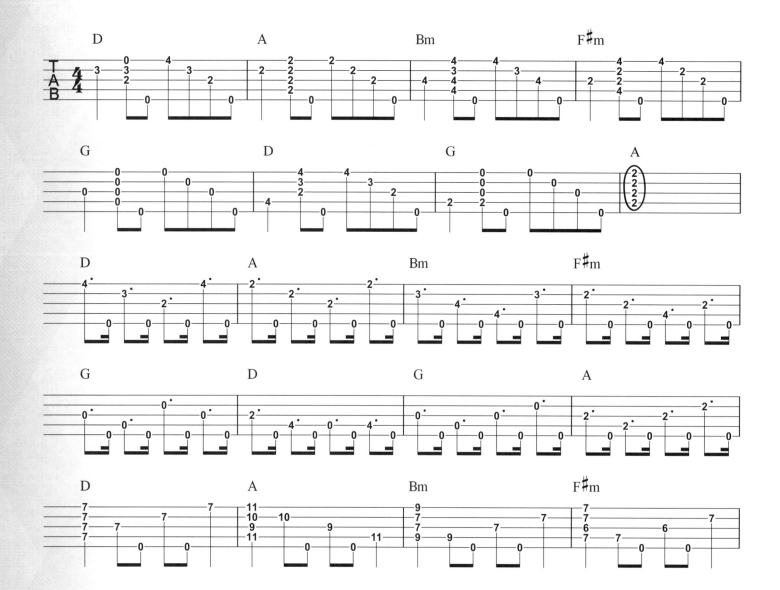

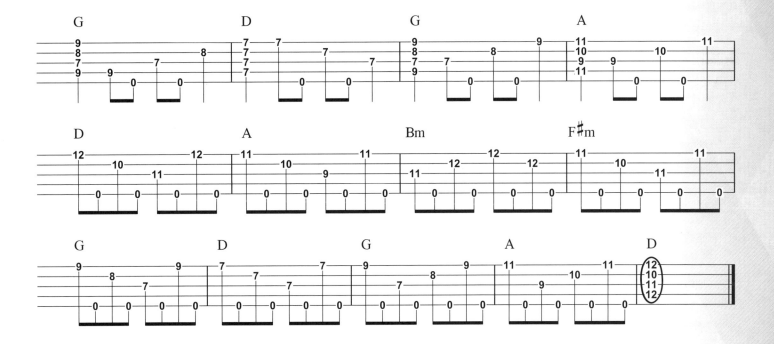

★ CHAPTER 12 ★
EXOTIC FLAVORS (WORLD MUSIC)

Yes, banjo is an American instrument. And yes, banjo is usually thought of as a country music instrument. Clawhammer banjo is generally associated with the music of the Southern states. But the banjo's delightful, bouncy sound—along with clawhammer's steady backbeat—lends well to all sorts of music from many different places.

It's fairly common these days to play Irish, Scottish, and English music clawhammer style. So for this chapter, we'll steer clear of the British Isles and visit a few other parts of the world. This short chapter in no way comes close to covering the subject of world music on the banjo. It's barely a taste. But I hope it's enough to prove the concept and maybe inspire you to go looking for new things to play on your banjo.

MIXING MUSIC AND METAPHORS

There are always many ways to approach any tune, and possibilities multiply when you're mixing styles. Using the cooking metaphor, you can consider the tune to be the food—for this example, let's say it's a gelatin dessert—and the clawhammer style is the mold. Whatever you pour into the mold will come out shaped like the mold. In other words, you can force the tune into the clawhammer mold. It'll still be the tune inside, and it's a great way to combine styles (if that's the sound you want). You may want to play an old-time Southern-sounding version of a tune from another style or country. I often do when I'm looking for material for my old-time string band.

But if you want to play banjo with slack key guitarists, a belly dance band, a Mariachi band, a Gypsy Jazz Hot Club, a reggae band, or any of a hundred other groups, you'll want to change your playing style enough to blend in with the existing style. The key word here is *blend*, and the cooking metaphor is to throw it all into the blender. Both the tune and the style will be reshaped, but they'll be well-mixed together. It's still a banjo. It won't sound like a slack key guitar, oud, bouzouki, or jazz guitar. The goal is to maintain the banjo's individuality yet fit into the existing style enough that you don't throw off (or piss off) the other players and/or listeners. If you're playing their music with them, it's up to you to fit in. To experiment with this, we'll be breaking out of the bum-ditty rhythms in some of these tunes. Don't be surprised if your fifth string feels neglected now and then!

ALOHA 'OE

This song, written by Queen Lili'uokalani in the late 1870s, has been sung and played by millions, ranging from the great Hawaiian traditional players to Elvis Presley. We could speed it up and turn the melody into a bouncy fiddle tune, but instead, let's take advantage of a chance to show that the banjo—even clawhammer banjo—can sound sweet and pretty. If you play it right, you'll feel the ocean breeze in your hair and sand between your toes.

One way to approach this song is with a straight melody, as shown on the top line, which can be sung or played on any instrument (including banjo), and a simple clawhammer chord back-up, as shown on the bottom line. Don't let the 16th notes scare you. This song is played slowly enough that you'll actually be playing your bum-ditties slower than usual.

This is played in open G tuning, which is very similar to the Taro Patch slack key guitar tuning. I've shown only one verse and one chorus, so repeat as needed for the whole song. (On the audio, only the chord back-up is played.)

TRACK 14

0:00

Aloha 'Oe
(straight melody and simple chords)

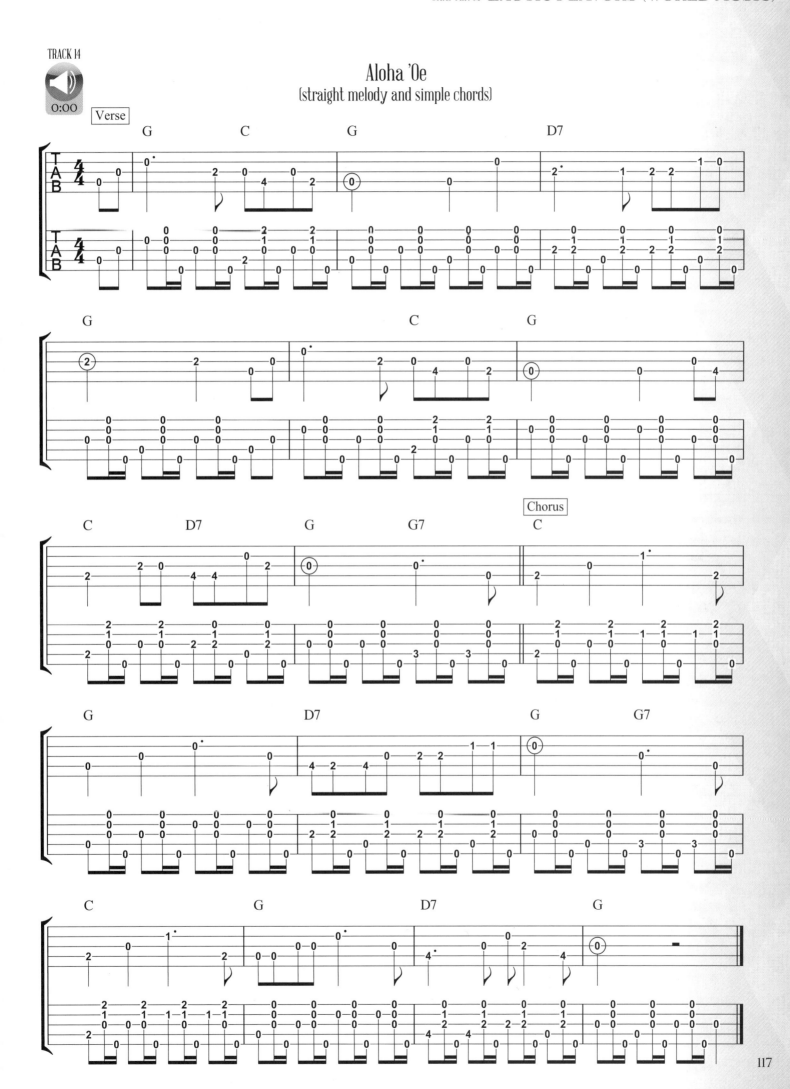

Here's another arrangement of "Aloha 'Oe" that uses the usual clawhammer techniques to combine the melody and chords.

TRACK 14

1:23

Aloha 'Oe
(combined chords and melody)

HOPAK KASATSKE

Now we move from Hawaii to Eastern Europe for a fast, fun Klezmer tune. A *hopak* is a Ukrainian folk dance, so we're really international now. This is a fast, high-energy dance, so banjo is right at home.

It's played here in open G tuning. The A section is in the key of G, and the B section is in the key of C. I've shown a basic melody here, and it'll take a while to get up to speed. Traditionally, though, Klezmer music is played with a lot of improvisation and ornamentation, so once you can play this comfortably, see what variations you can come up with.

TRACK 14

2:47

Hopak Kasatske

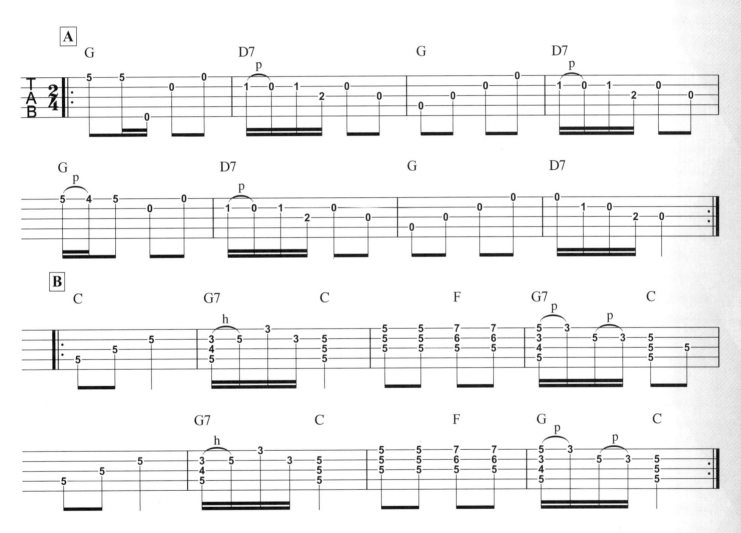

ES EL AMOR MARIPOSA

"Es el Amor Mariposa" is a Mexican tango. Take it slowly and try to keep the rhythm steady.

3:15

Es el Amor Mariposa

Tuning: aDGBD

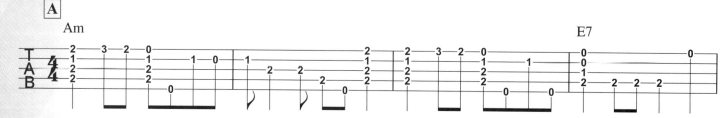

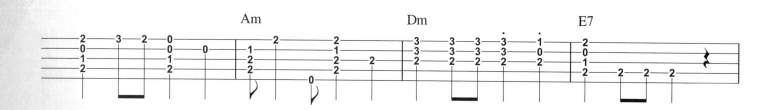

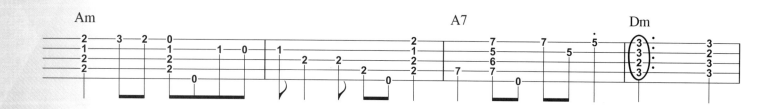

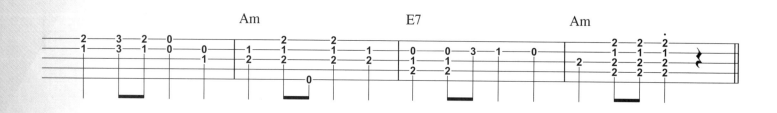

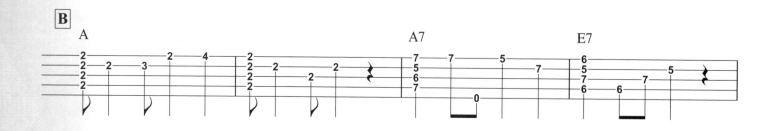

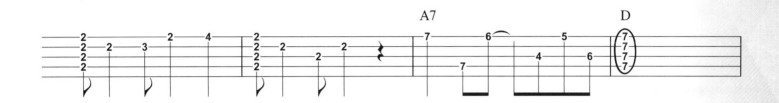

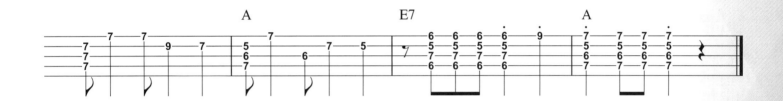

★ CHAPTER 13 ★
DESSERTS

Nothing caps off a good meal like a sweet treat; I'm talking about dessert here. Of course, some may prefer coffee and brandy, but that's for another book. A musical dessert is something that's fun—both to play and to hear. Here are some fun techniques that you can use in lots of different pieces.

DOUBLE STOPS: 6THS

Double stops are pairs of notes that sound good together. They can be played at the same time or one after the other. Guitarists use them a lot, especially with slides, as in this Hawaiian lick.

TRACK 15

0:00

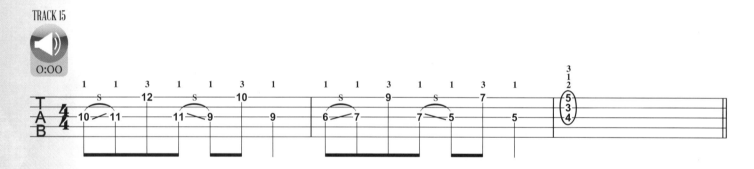

The double stops in the Hawaiian lick are 6ths. Here are a few demonstration exercises that show how to play 6ths in a more clawhammer-ish way. The first one stays low on the neck.

TRACK 15

0:10

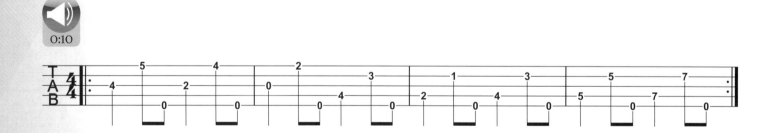

This next one goes all the way up the neck on the first and third strings.

TRACK 15

0:24

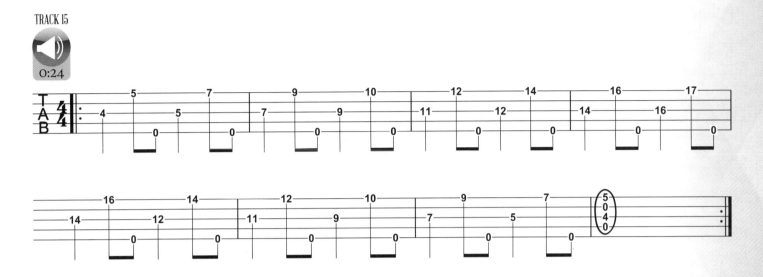

This one goes up and down the neck on the second and fourth strings.

TRACK 15

0:45

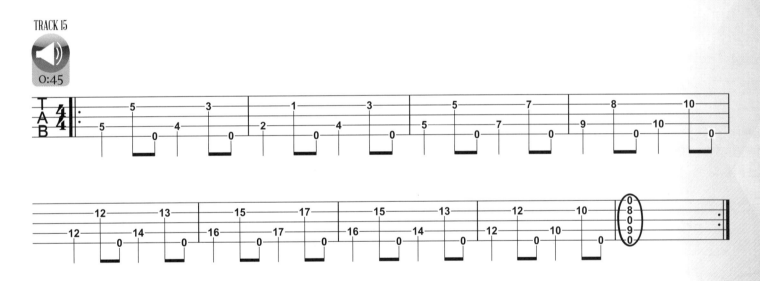

These examples are exercises that are very scale-like. Once you have a feel for them, start using them to make music. Play with them, add slides, and make up licks. Use them to fancy-up a simple melody that you like.

DOUBLE STOPS: 3RDS

Another dish of ear candy is double stops made out of 3rds. Here's a scaly introduction that takes you all over the neck. The example shows one note at a time, but since the two notes are on adjacent strings, you may be able to brush them. Give it a try.

TRACK 15

1:08

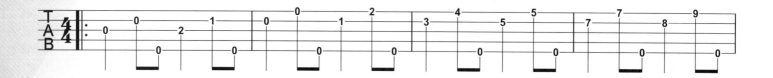

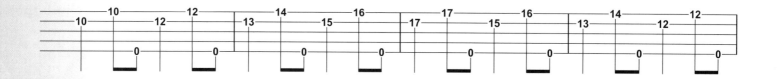

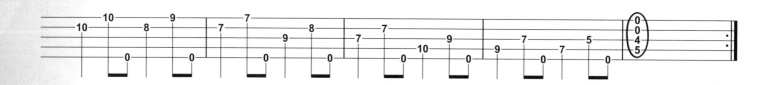

I'm supplying some potentially tasty ingredients here; it's up to you to turn this into music!

DOUBLE STOPS: OCTAVES

Another popular double stop is the octave. On banjo in open G tuning, the only way to play them is to fret the first and fourth strings at the same fret. To play both notes at the same time, you'll have to strike with a "double-claw." I like to use the index and ring fingers. To play them one at a time, you can use your usual striking finger, but since the strings are so far apart, you may want to try to use two striking fingers. Again, I like to use the index and ring for this.

We already did a little octave work in one of the variations of "Shady Grove," but here's a simple scale shown with both individual and simultaneous notes.

TRACK 15

1:40

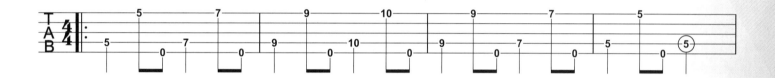

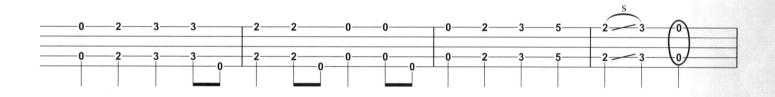

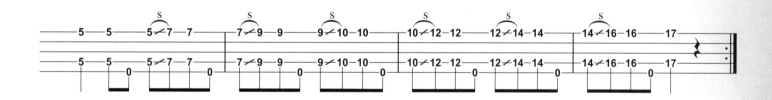

TWO-STRING CHORDS WITH DRONE

Here's another fun take on double stops that uses just the second and third strings to make chords and melody. The first, fourth, and fifth strings can be droned along to give this technique a nice sound.

   The tab may look complicated, but it's really not. First play the first measure; it's open strings, so all the work is done by the striking hand. In all the other measures (except for the last one), the striking hand plays the exact same pattern, and the fretting hand only plays on strings 2 and 3.

TRACK 15

2:08

Try it with as many other different striking-hand patterns as you can think of and then improvise different melodies with your fretting hand. Heck, try strumming it; I know it's not clawhammer, but I won't tell!

FINAL WORDS

Ok, so if you made it all the way here, that means you've spent some time on the rest of the book, learning the techniques and understanding how to apply them to any tune you want to play. You know more about your instrument and the fretboard than when you started, and you're ready to move forward and use everything you've learned to develop your own individual style of clawhammer playing—and to have some serious big fun playing music!

Then again, you might be one of those people who reads the last pages of a book first. If you are, then... SPOILER ALERT! The banjo player did it! Or you will (I hope).

Seriously, I really want this book to be helpful to banjo players. I want it to help you better understand your instrument so you can play more and have more fun with it. While we all respect and treasure clawhammer's traditions, I want you to see that there is room for new traditions, and that the clawhammer style of playing is a viable technique for many musical styles. If you have any questions, or need any clarification, I'll be supporting this book at **banjoged.com**.

Thank you, and have a great musical life. Now get out there and play some music!

Michael Bremer
Grass Valley, CA

ACKNOWLEDGMENTS

I'd like to thank the fine people at Hal Leonard for this opportunity and their support. I'd like to thank my family for putting up with my noise for decades, and especially my wife, Linda, who has to listen to my banjo every day. I thank Tom Ferkel and Michael Singletary for filling my formative years with music (including my first band) and still giving me a place to sleep and a night of jamming whenever I'm in town. My thanks also go out to all my current band members in the Buffalo Gals, Rush Creek, and Sgt. Funky. I also send a shout-out to the many people I play music and jam with, including the Mountain Fiddlers, the Dutch Flat Old-Time Jam, and the Nevada County Banjo Summit. A real big thanks is reserved for the next venue that hires me to play.

And now for a bit of blame: six or seven years ago, I took a workshop from the great teacher and banjo player, Cathy Fink. I learned a lot in that class and had a good time. It was at a time when I was just starting to experiment with playing outside the lines of strict traditional music. I don't remember the exact words, but she said something to the effect of, "It's music. You're enjoying it. It's good." Whether she meant to or not, she gave me (or I took) permission to break rules, mix styles, and have my way with the banjo, which led, among other places, to this book.

Thanks, Cathy.

ABOUT THE AUTHOR

Michael Bremer makes his living through words, music, and teaching. As a writer, editor, and publisher, he has worked on projects ranging from computer games to medical equipment to online math courses to music instruction. As a musician, he has played guitar since 1968. In 2002, he moved to the Sierra Nevada foothills in Northern California and decided it was time to learn banjo. It took over his musical world. Today, he plays banjo (and guitar) in a number of bands that play everything from old-time to swing to rock and roll (yes, he plays electric banjo in a rock band—but don't tell the California Bluegrass Association). He also writes songs and believes it's time for banjo to re-enter the world of singer-songwriters. Through it all, Michael is a compulsive teacher, holding workshops and seminars for writers as well as banjo players, and has taught classes at the California Bluegrass Association Music Camp. Combining his instructional writing, his love of music (especially banjo), and teaching, he began writing and producing a series of instructional books and videos, which is what brought him to the attention of Hal Leonard and led to this book.

Michael supports this book, answers questions, provides clarification, and, when possible, additional information at **banjoged.com**.